ALCHEMY OF BECOMING

A JOURNEY TO FINDING THE ONE

By Pritam Atma

Copyright © 2021 by Pritam Atma

All rights reserved. No part of this publication may be reproduced, distributed, or transmitted in any form or by any means, including photocopying, recording, or other electronic or mechanical methods, without the prior written permission of the publisher, except in the case of brief quotations embodied in critical reviews and certain other noncommercial uses permitted by copyright law. For permission requests, write to the publisher, addressed "Attention: Permissions Coordinator," at the address below.

ISBN Print: 978-0-578-88483-7
ISBN eBook: 978-0-578-88482-0

Printed in the United States of America

Table of Contents

ABOUT THE AUTHOR   8
INTRODUCTION: CONNECTING TO THE HEART   11

CHAPTER ONE: THE HERO'S JOURNEY   21

DEAR DAD   21
DEATH AND THE HERO'S JOURNEY   23
A JOURNEY TO INDIA   26
A CALL TO ACTION   29
THE ENERGETIC SHIFT   32
DO WE CHOOSE OUR PARENTS?   36
IDENTIFYING FAMILY TEMPLATES   38
THE ORIGINAL WOUNDS WITHIN YOUR RELATIONSHIPS   41
ALCHEMY: THE STEPS TO HEALING   49

CHAPTER TWO: CALCINATION   53

STEP INTO THE FIRE   53
A STORY OF CALCINATION   56
DARKNESS   64
FEAR   70

CHAPTER THREE: DISSOLUTION   75

OPENING THE FLOODGATES   75
TRAUMA BONDING IN RELATIONSHIPS   80
FORGIVE AND FORGET   82

CHAPTER FOUR: SEPARATION — 87

GETTING TO KNOW YOURSELF — 87
NOTICING THE RED FLAGS — 89
AVOIDING POTENTIALLY DANGEROUS RELATIONSHIPS — 91
SEPARATING FROM THE PAIN — 93
HOW TO BEGIN HEALING — 97

CHAPTER FIVE: CONJUNCTION — 101

COMING TOGETHER — 101
STEPS TO BECOMING WHOLE — 103
GROWING UP — 107
EXPERIENCING POLARITIES — 109

CHAPTER SIX: FERMENTATION AND PUTREFACTION — 115

THE POWER OF IMAGINATION — 115
THE ILLUSIONS OF THE EGO — 117
MANIFESTING FROM THE MIND — 118
STOPPING SELF-SABOTAGE — 123

CHAPTER SEVEN: DISTILLATION — 127

YOUR DEEPEST DESIRES — 127
LET GO AND LET GOD — 129
THE SIKH MAN — 131
THE EAST COAST PREPPY MAN — 133
SURRENDER — 135

CHAPTER EIGHT: COAGULATION — 141

A LEGACY OF LOVE	141
MOVING INTO PRESENCE	145
BECOMING WHOLE	149
AWAKENING TO SOVEREIGNTY	151
YOUR JOURNEY BACK HOME	153
WORKS CITED	157
END NOTES	158

DEDICATION

I dedicate this book to all the women that have been searching for true love.

The single mothers. The mothers who stay with men that are mentally, physically, and emotionally absent. I honor your resilience. The women who are abused and mistreated. I salute the ones who stay and I acknowledge the ones that leave. I tell you all: the only way to feel the love that you have been searching for in a partner is to heal your heart. You will resurrect your soul and move out of the darkness of your mind. By doing this, you will find The One you have been looking for the whole time — yourself.

I dedicate this book to my teachers from The Golden Chain and the Divine Feminine Ascended Masters that have led me each step of the way. With deep gratitude, I honor my teachers Celestine Star, Elizabeth Burke, and Guru Jagat. With all of my heart, thank you for taking me through the journey back home. Also, I thank Amber Loveland, my beloved sister, for your many hours of continuous support through my healing.

About the Author

Pritam Atma (previously named Chelsea Ann Wiley) wrote *Alchemy of Becoming* as a part of the *Mystical Motherhood* book series. Her first books focused on motherhood and include: *Mystical Motherhood: Create a Happy and Conscious Family: A Guidebook for Conception, Pregnancy, Birth, and Beyond* and *Fertile: Prepare Your Body, Mind, and Spirit for Conception and Pregnancy to Create a Conscious Child*. She is deeply connected to bringing conscious children into this world. She currently works as a Nurse Practitioner in a fertility center in the New York area, practicing Reproductive Medicine. Pritam Atma also works with women privately and in groups, helping them to apply the concepts of her books to increase their fertility and consciously prepare themselves for motherhood. All of her courses, books, and podcasts can be found at:

www.mysticalmotherhood.com

Facebook: Mystical Motherhood

Instagram: @mysticalmotherhood

Podcast: *Mystical Motherhood*

She has also worked as a labor and delivery nurse at the top medical center in the US: the University of California, San Francisco, and studied with Ina May Gaskin, the most famous midwife in the world. She is a board-certified Family Nurse Practitioner (FNP) and a Kundalini Yoga and Meditation teacher. At the hospital and in the primary care clinic, she found that families were unprepared for birth and parenting, that they lacked knowledge to maintain health, and yearned for a deeper understanding of how to integrate spiritual practices into daily life. Pritam Atma envisions raising the consciousness of families around the globe and changing the frequency of the women who bring children into this world so that the next generation can live as peaceful, vibrant, and healthy individuals. She wrote this book for mothers, as she is a mother herself and knows that this population will change the world as we know it.

INTRODUCTION: CONNECTING TO THE HEART

We all have a story, and what we refer to as our "story" is just a perception of reality based on the interpretation of our mind. Many chapters of our story are unpleasant, some a little more than others, and they have things in common — they lack love and take away our energy. What if I told you that none of it was real and that you could let go of the painful stories you tell yourself about your life by tapping into your heart? In the process of letting your deepest wounds go lies the gold of your being — it reveals the light of your consciousness, which is what our planet desperately needs at this time.

It is absolutely essential that we begin to let go of the drama and trauma of our wounds so that we can heal individually and collectively. Most of humanity is lacking self-love and connection to the heart. The way that each person deals with this is different and is based on their conditioning from childhood. Throughout the book, I will refer to this conditioning as *original wounds*, which is the human story that we carry around and repeat throughout our life even if it hurts us. This story usually stems from our childhood memories or the subconscious programming completed while we were in utero, and we may not even be consciously aware that we are recreating pain in our relationships. These wounds are any disruptive experiences that have not met resolution. They defeat us by creating a low vibrational frequency that keeps us stuck within our old patterns. We then repeat the past and complain about the present.

The process of healing is one of alchemical transformation that changes your life forever. I know this because I have been through it and have documented my journey here for you. The fastest way to awaken is to help someone else and the only way to do this is tell your story so that others can know that it is possible to change their life narrative too. Awakening is the process of letting go of the human story of pain — which closes our hearts and takes over our minds — so that we can connect to our Divine Self and become sovereign human beings.

I dedicated this book specifically to the healing of our wounds around intimate relationships because this is where pain commonly arises. It is through intimate relationship with another human being that we can clearly see ourselves and all the ways that we have diverged from love. Personally, I compensated for my lack of self-love through the search of love from men that could not provide it. You may search for this love through magnifying different insecurities within you or inflating your ego to make yourself feel greater. No matter what your conditioning is, this book will help you heal, because every relationship that you have is preparation for having a relationship with yourself. This is the most important one. On a search for your destination, you will take a road back home to you — and each encounter with another is leading you there.

I wrote my first two books *Mystical Motherhood* and *Fertile* to help women heal their mother wound so that they can become better mothers themselves. *Alchemy of Becoming* is dedicated to healing the father aspect within each individual and the patriarchal structure of humanity as a whole. This system is built on action, material growth, power, and control. This system is being dismantled and the only way for us to adjust to living in a more peace-filled manner is to learn how to heal any distortions within ourselves. The healing of the male and female aspects, or the mother and father wounds, will help you to become a whole human being who is happy, content, and contained. You have less desire to look to your external environment for well-being — you recognize that it is completely out of your control.

My original wound is described in this book as the pain I associated with my father. It was the story I was unconsciously playing out in my life, and it held me back from experiencing worthiness, joy, self-love, awareness, and God. The process of alchemical transformation that I went through to heal was miraculous. The journey took me from the Himalayas, through Scotland, Ireland, around Mary Magdalene's land in France, to the sacred sites of England and Egypt. I embarked on the hero's journey, embodying historical archetypes and healing generations of patterns through my alchemical transformation.

The most remarkable aspect of my journey is that I did not consciously know what was happening until I made it out the other side. There is tremendous growth and internal power that is generated through the chaos of not knowing, as it requires you to be present with what is happening now. Like Alice after she fell down the rabbit hole and woke up from a dream, I asked myself if everything I had experienced was real. When I returned to a regular life, everything was different, yet it was all the same. The most significant change was that I had let go of my human story and connected to Spirit or God. I learned that in order have any relationship succeed, the flow of the infinite Spirit needs to exist within you first.

My original wound was associated with my father and the childhood conditioning that I had to release in order to heal. This was a story that I kept repeating with every man I became intimate with. The wound distorted my entire reality, took over my thought stream and didn't allow me to experience the radiant love of my heart. I was focused on the pain that was reflected back to me through these relationships. My thoughts were constantly focused on "him" in whatever form "he" came, which was always just another aspect of the love I never received.

The healing of my thought stream allowed the opening of my heart. I spent my life searching for love through a man, and it took a transformation to find out that I am that love. I found that no man or external experience can give me the happiness that I am seeking. Once you identify your original wound, and how it has hijacked your life, you will be able to see how letting it go is the road back to yourself. Your wounds distort your reality and stop you from moving towards your destiny because so much of your energy is wasted on the pain of the past.

In this book, I am not asking you to deeply explore the emotions and commotions of your past. I will only request that you recognize that these patterns exist and that they hold you back as they play out in your present relationships. I will encourage you to use various spiritual technologies to transform yourself and move on to live your best life and serve others. Successful people have a connection to a higher force, rather than to the mental emotions held within the human body. This is your quest. Your original wounds, or childhood conditioning, may be similar to mine or very different. What matters is that you are ready to let that conditioning go so that you can live your best life, and create a more conscious relationship with anyone around you. This is the journey of the alchemist — a journey back to the heart.

The alchemical process I will describe in this book is what humanity will go through on an individual and global scale as all of our hearts open over the coming years. The only way for this to happen is to heal. Whether the wounds are based on race, finances, sex, abuse, war crimes, drugs or alcohol, it is time that we heal our planet. As the heart opens, the individual will have to experience what caused the heart to close in the first place. This process will help each person to identify and release the wounds that made the energetic center of love contract. When you are not connected to your heart, or your center of neutrality and Christ Consciousness, you are essentially living from your mind, which creates duality. This state of polarity creates tension through contradicting tendencies which take you away from being neutral and present.

As you go through your alchemical transformation and heart-opening experience, the people in your life and events in your external environment will help you to process your pain by playing out the conditioning of your past. This is always happening, but as the pressure for more people to awaken increases on the planet, it is now in your best interest to be cognizant that it is actually occurring. More alchemists are needed on Earth — now more than ever to transmute, purify, and perfect themselves. Understanding the steps of alchemy will put you on a higher playing field.

As you learn about each of these stages, you will be able to navigate where you are in life and change your narrative. There is power in altering your story, especially if you are the first in your family to do so. *Alchemy of Becoming* creates a template for you to heal your wounds through personal transformation. This alchemical process was brought to Earth through the Emerald Tablet by the god Thoth in ancient Egypt; I will discuss the Tablet in detail later in the book.

The stages of alchemy are described in more significant detail in Dennis Hauck's book *The Emerald Tablet: Alchemy of Personal Transformation*. These steps are happening to everyone all of the time, but most individuals cannot make it past the first few stages of purification. There is an urgency to awaken and choose love over fear. The latter is only a living nightmare of your own making. Alchemists tend to go on this journey at an accelerated pace, and if you are reading this, you are one of them. Identifying your wounds and moving through the alchemical transformation to experience higher love is the path of the spiritual warrior. The Universe is not here to serve you — you are here to serve the Universe. Through this process of letting go and merging, you will find The ONE that you have been looking for all along.

The steps of transformation are experienced as follows:

There is only one Pattern in the Operation of the Sun. By Fire you will be set free; by Water you will reclaim your power. By Air you will discover your inner worth; by Earth you will realize its potential. In its Dissolution you will see the Pattern encompassing you and know what to do, for this

Pattern originated with the birth of the universe and is sealed in time and space everywhere. Only then will you be allowed to contribute to the universe; only then will the child of your imagination be allowed to grow. — **Dennis Hauck**

Calcination: This phase breaks down your attachment to the material world; it is the phase of the destruction of delusions, appearances, and possessions. The element fire burns away the mental constructs and belief systems that hold you back and box you in.

Dissolution: This phase reveals unconscious emotional parts of yourself for release. The element water is used to dissolve heavy feelings and negative thoughts. Unresolved wounds of the heart will arise to be healed.

Separation: In this phase, you begin taking an intimate look at your personality, deciding what parts of yourself that you want to separate from and what parts need further integration. The element air helps with this process by making changes in your physical, emotional, and mental realms. The element helps to quickly release old ways of being. You will consciously review your unconscious and decide if you are ready to release the blockages, phobias, and neurotic tendencies — or not.

Conjunction: This is the phase where you merge the conscious and the unconscious parts of yourself for deeper healing. The element earth begins to build a new reality within your consciousness and a different way to experience the world which is more stable and balanced. It is the union of the masculine and feminine within. Your heart begins to open and your intuition grows as you become connected to Spirit.

Fermentation and Putrefaction: This is the introduction into your new life. You will experience a death of your old world and be initiated into a new way of being. The element ether begins to arise within your consciousness as you move through the final three phases of the alchemical process. Ether helps you to ascend into the higher realms and begin to see that the reality on Earth is actually connected to a previously unseen and unheard world. As a spiritual warrior, you begin to hear the call to help others along the way.

Distillation: In order to know whether you can hold true in this new life, you will be psychologically tested by a higher force. This phase of purification is agitating to the human mind as there must be no impure or negative subconscious thoughts affecting the personality in order to enter a state of peace.

Coagulation: The whole and healed human being is rare, but if you have reached this stage, you are now fully conscious and interacting with the world from the level of the heart or with love. Being becomes as important as doing. You will see the world from a new perspective and higher level of consciousness. This is the rise of the Phoenix and the phase of resurrection into your highest destiny.

CHAPTER ONE: THE HERO'S JOURNEY

DEAR DAD

Dear Dad,

Though I was there when you were buried, you never died. I found you in every male I became intimate with until I healed. Everywhere I looked, there you were. Your mental illness was the driving force of my life. I wanted so badly to heal you in order to feel your love, and though I failed at this, the journey was successful because I learned to find that love within myself.

I studied every psychological disorder in school so that I would be prepared to attempt to help every male I came across in order to become closer to you. I spent my life trying to heal your broken and manic mind. I lived in fear of your reactions and found solace in men that exhibited your absence because they were never quite able to be mentally, emotionally or physically present with me. I was accustomed to chaos because it made me feel safe. Each man I picked mirrored a different aspect of the love I always needed from you and could never quite tangibly feel or receive. When these men did not give me the love I desired, I became manic just like you. Like father, like daughter. The cycle repeated.

In every partner that I "chose" were elements of you, found within me, that were reflected back through them. You essentially arranged my partnerships without my conscious consent. Every disagreement I ever had was never really with them. I was only trying to get through to you. I was looking for your love all along.

It took me almost a decade to heal this, to heal my heart, and move out of the human story of pain. I can see clearly now that I never got a fair chance at starting a healthy relationship. I had to learn the hard way what healthy love meant and how to find this within myself. Because I did not receive that template or program, I had to design one. If I can help just one woman change this for herself and the next generation, then all that I went through is worthwhile.

I write this letter for all individuals who will read this book, in hopes that the path to the resurrection of my heart will serve as a path for all of you to find yours. If I could personally speak to every individual who has been looking for a partner in the wrong person, I would tell you to look no further than the relationship you had with your parents.

DEATH AND THE HERO'S JOURNEY

Death comes in many forms: fear, darkness, destruction of ego, experiencing your soul leaving the body or death of a loved one. Death is a catalyst for your greatest awakening and creates immense change in life. Learn to embrace it, as it is part of the first stage of alchemy and an essential element in your journey to awakening. As an alchemist who has gone through the alchemical transformation that will be described in detail throughout this book, my father's death brought on one of the biggest transformations in my life.

I wasn't sad when my father died; I don't remember crying one tear or having the faintest moment of remorse. In fact, I was the one who made the final decision to take him off life support and — I have to be honest — that wasn't a very hard decision for me at all. The transformational process that followed his death required me to let go of ingrained generational trauma and forced me to heal my original wounds. The healing of this trauma will hopefully change your life too, as it birthed the creation of this book.

An alchemist has many stories. These stories are nothing short of miracles combining pain, pleasure, truth, and a profound connection to Source, Spirit or God. Every alchemist knows that Spirit runs the show. In order to begin the hero's journey, each adept, or alchemist in training, will go through a series of initiations to accelerate the healing of their heart. This journey is never logical, because one cannot learn to hear the unheard or see the unseen through the mind. It is from the heart that life's decisions to complete the soul's mission come.

The initiations that an alchemist goes through help to reveal the destiny. According to Guru Jagat, a teacher of Kundalini Yoga and Meditation, when you begin living an incarnational destiny, you are always in the right place at the right time. Most individuals do not know what their incarnational destiny is because they cannot remember what they came to Earth to do. For some, this experience creates a feeling of being lost, which then manifests as a longing within to connect back to God.

Almost everyone comes to the planet with a mission to complete, but because of the *density* of their original wounds, it is hard to remember or become focused on what this *destiny* actually is (your energetic density blocks your destiny). The only way to change this is to create a new frequency through spiritual technologies. When you are on the path of living your incarnational destiny, you become connected to your soul's purpose and begin to accelerate through life by breaking glass ceilings and creating a legacy of love that others can follow so they can find their purpose too.

Fate is a word that can be used to describe the energetic density that blocks you from completing what you came here to do. Guru Jagat explained that living a story of fate will put you consistently in the wrong place at the wrong time. Fate is controlled not only by your original wounds, but also by your karmic past, ancestral heritage, and planetary placements at the time of your birth. (These are all connected.) The spiritual technologies mentioned in this book, including the steps of alchemical transformation and Kundalini Yoga and Meditation, will help you leave a path of fate and move into you're your highest soul's purpose. Your free will gives you the right to do so.

As your highest mission unfolds, you will place yourself in a new life narrative, which will be completely different from that of your friends, family or past. You will play out ancient stories and become archetypes for your own healing. This requires a great amount of energy, power, and sovereignty. Guru Jagat taught me that the higher the destiny you are living, the more you will experience hyper-synchronicity. What follows is a story of just that, and it begins before my father's death. The journey of alchemical transformation is never logical, so please read this book though your heart's eyes.

A JOURNEY TO INDIA

When I decided to return to India, I had already been on the path to self-healing for almost seven years, but I still had a lot of growth ahead of me. I understood what fate meant only by the loneliness and longing I felt within my body to find my soul's purpose. I did not quite understand what it meant to be on the path of destiny — yet. A week or so before my planned third trip to India, I was deep in meditation during the early morning hours in a cottage I was living in, in Dublin, Ireland. I had moved there from California with my husband and two children for his business. On this particular day, something odd happened and I met my father's energy in my third eye, or the place between the eyebrows that is similar to a movie theatre when one looks up and inside with one's eyes closed. We engaged in a beautiful celestial soul dance in the Spirit world and went through an energetic life review, which led us to a mutual understanding and deep forgiveness of the past. In my mind's eye, I began to fly with my father through the heavens, and I left him at some very large gates. After forty-five minutes, I came out of this experience feeling calm and peaceful and I did not think much about it again.

As an alchemist, I should have known that "as above, so below" always applies. This means that earthly matters are a reflection of what happens in the higher planes and what takes place in these dimensions also affects Earth. On the same day I was leaving for India, I received a call from my sister. I was about to take an expedition to liberate seventeen generations of my family (no small feat but a necessary incarnational destiny upgrade). She told me that our father was in the hospital on life support because he had recently fallen down in the garage and severely injured himself. I asked when this occurred and found that it was the exact same time that I had been in meditation with him days before — when I had left him at the Gates of Heaven. He was not ready to pass through them yet for reasons I did not yet understand.

I asked my sister if she wanted me to fly home to help and explained that I would skip my trip to India. She told me to go directly there and made me realize that there was nothing that I could do to help him. She was right: I had tried to help my father function and heal for most of my life. My father suffered from bipolar disorder and schizophrenia. The bipolar disorder created severe manic episodes with contrasting catatonic depression later in his life. His diagnosis of schizophrenia gave him the ability to hear voices speaking to him (not the angelic ones). His severe disabilities made him unpredictable, dangerous, and incredibly frightening to grow up around.

It was a huge relief when my sister gave me permission to keep running away from my past. I had been running from home since I was eighteen and had traveled most of the world to get as far away as I could. Like Dorothy, I always wanted to go home, but I couldn't quite find where it was located. This caused a great dis-ease within me as I never felt comfortable in my external or internal environments. There was a drive to find that peace through people, places, and experiences outside myself, which were always just reflections of my internal struggle and chaos. Just like Alice in Wonderland, it felt natural to live in a world that was outside the norm of reality.

Alice in Wonderland and Dorothy from Oz are just a couple of the archetypal figures that provide great examples of the hero's journey. This type of narrative creates a common template for us to follow to find ourselves. It involves a hero who goes on an adventure, meets a crisis only to overcome it and comes out transformed. There are a series of stages that the hero or alchemist must go through on the journey. The story begins with the adept living in a normal world, totally oblivious of the adventure he or she is about to embark on. There is then a call to action and adventure which the adept politely refuses. In order to push the adept into incarnational destiny, a teacher or mentor will appear to help the individual cross the threshold and conquer his or her inner demons. During the journey, tests, allies, and enemies appear. These hurdles teach the adept who is trustworthy and he or she gains insight into human character.

In order to make it through this difficult journey, the adept must go inside to find the courage to continue. This period is the final preparation before a physical test or crisis takes place in the adept's life, at which point the original wounds of the past can resurface to be healed once and for all. A metaphysical death occurs that will eventually transform the adept into the alchemist, who is resurrected and rewarded with a new life. Ultimately, the alchemist will return to his or her normal world again, but as a transformed human being carrying the philosopher's stone or secret elixir of transformation. The hero's journey encompasses the stages of alchemy, and when completed, things are never again the same.

A CALL TO ACTION

When my father was in the hospital, I was still an adept at the beginning of the narrative and not aware I was about to begin the hero's journey. Living a regular life in a calm and secure manner always felt foreign to me. Just like Alice, I knew there was something greater — a world beyond this world. The boredom felt like unhealed irritability and general discomfort because I was not yet delivering what I came to Earth to do. I was living a life of fate and not destiny. I fell down the rabbit hole when I arrived in Amristar, India and descended down the stairs of liberation.

Amristar, near the border of Pakistan, holds the steps of Goindwal. This is a sacred site that millions of Sikh pilgrims visit every year. I, with a large group of friends, had prepared for this trip for almost three years by reciting the Japji prayer daily. The Japji is a Sikh prayer which holds all of heavenly reality within its sound current; it is pronounced in Gurmukhi, the Sikh script, and takes about thirty-four minutes to recite. With practice, the prayer can be reduced in time and recited with greater ease.

This Sikh shrine was constructed in the sixteenth century by Guru Amar Das. At the site there are eighty-four covered steps, divided for male and female devotees, that descend into the Earth to a sacred well of naturally collected rain water. Each step represents 100,000 life forms of a possible 8.4

million incarnational existences. In order to liberate him or herself, and seventeen generations forwards and backwards combined, the devotee must recite the Japji prayer on each step starting from the bottom of the staircase. After each step, he or she must descend to the well and submerge fully in the water three times before moving up to the next stair to recite the prayer again.

The actual event is mentally, physically, emotionally, and spiritually exhausting. It feels like being torn open. Similar to childbirth. Equal to three full-blown marathons, but you are soaking wet the whole time. Everything inside screams "Get out!" yet your body persists in overcoming the mind as you continually descend and ascend the stairs. This is what alchemists live for — the transformation.

The night before I completed the Goindwal stairs, I dreamt I was walking in another dimensional time where a blackbird began to fly towards me. I could not tell if I was awake or sleeping when my alarm went off to begin my morning Sadhana, or meditations, that start around 4 a.m. I quickly shut it off, reminding myself that I would be praying all day on the stairs and needed my rest. To my surprise, the blow-dryer in the bathroom of the room I was staying in suddenly turned on, which was my signal from God that I had no choice but to get up and get my act together through prayer. I had to pray to play.

When I walked down to meet my friends to start our meditations, I told them about the blackbird in my dream and asked what it meant. They told me to use the vision on the stairs somehow, as it was obviously a gift. Later that day we headed to the stairs and began our descent into the well. And, just like Alice as she fell into the rabbit hole, my vision began to change. I was reciting the Japji prayer and was reminded of the blackbird. I suddenly knew what do. I began to flap the blackbird's wings in my mind's eye which gave me the energy of flight. To my surprise, I began to channel the prayer without having to read the words. My timing also dropped and I recited it in approximately ten minutes instead of thirty-four (normally, it requires years of practice to get to this point).

When I finished the stairs, I was beyond delusional and felt like I was outside my body, yet on Earth. I had prayed from sundown to after sunrise the next day without a single break. After, I returned to my hotel room to sleep. When I woke up, I took a walk around the Golden Temple in Amristar. The Golden Temple is the energetic pineal gland of the planet, meaning it is interdimensional and connected to higher planes simultaneously. This sacred site, which is in a different location than the stairs, is one of the most stunning places on Earth. There are continuous prayers being sung in every room — devotees touch into divinity through all of their senses.

I was still curious what the significance of my blackbird vision was, both within my dream and on the stairs. Out of nowhere, a man walked up to me and began to tell a story. He pointed to a tree growing across the water from where I was standing and explained that it was the very sacred site where Guru Ram Das, the fourth Sikh Guru, received the vision to build the Golden Temple at this specific location in India. The man explained that Guru Ram Das saw a blackbird fly into the water and come out the color white. I asked him what that meant and he said, "Liberation of the mind," and walked away.

When the alchemist connects Heaven and Earth inside, he or she finds out that there is no difference between above and below. When you enter into the alchemical transformational process, your Higher Self begins to run your life. Everything becomes fully conscious and is a form of communication from Source. As an alchemist, you just have to trust that it is all real. All parts of your outer world will begin to speak to your inner world and vice versa. The mind becomes submissive to the heart's calling. When you awaken to this new Reality, your old way of Being can no longer exist. As an alchemist, your genetic line will disconnect from mass consciousness and when this happens, your entire life and all experiences will be different. Anything that is not good for your new state will eliminate itself.

THE ENERGETIC SHIFT

Shortly after I returned to Ireland from India, I received a call from my sister saying that my father had sepsis and was on life support. Since I was his eldest daughter, it was my decision to make as to whether or not he should be resuscitated. I called the hospital and said no, despite the negative feedback from my relatives. If he survived, he would have been incapacitated, or mentally and physically non-functional for the rest of his life. My father died that night.

A couple of days later, my aunt sent me the following poem which was a reflection of my father's name, Kevin. She told me that my father had been named after Saint Kevin. This was something I did not know at the time. It just so happened that Saint Kevin was an abbot at a sacred site in Ireland called Glendalough, which coincidentally was a forty-five-minute drive from where I was living in Dublin. The poem was written by Seamus Heaney.

And then there was St Kevin and the blackbird.
The saint is kneeling, arms stretched out, inside
His cell, but the cell is narrow, so

One turned-up palm is out the window, stiff
As a crossbeam, when a blackbird lands
And lays in it and settles down to nest.

Kevin feels the warm eggs, the small breast, the tucked
Neat head and claws and, finding himself linked
Into the network of eternal life,

Is moved to pity: now he must hold his hand
Like a branch out in the sun and rain for weeks
Until the young are hatched and fledged and flown.

And since the whole thing's imagined anyhow,
Imagine being Kevin. Which is he?
Self-forgetful or in agony all the time

From the neck on out down through his hurting forearms?
Are his fingers sleeping? Does he still feel his knees?
Or has the shut-eyed blank of underearth

Crept up through him? Is there distance in his head?
Alone and mirrored clear in love's deep river,
'To labour and not to seek reward,' he prays,

A prayer his body makes entirely
For he has forgotten self, forgotten bird
And on the riverbank forgotten the river's name.

 This poem brings great reflection to my father's life and our relationship. Heaney says, *"... now he must hold his hand. Like a branch out in the sun and rain for weeks. Until the young are hatched and fledged and flown."* My father was stuck, in agony, inside a body which was his cell most of his life until he died days after I completed the stairs of liberation. These stanzas make me wonder if he chose to be mentally ill so that I could play the role of the blackbird, link back into the network of life and liberate generations to come. Did his insanity push me to become self-reliant and find God? If this is true, my father Kevin, the man that terrorized me in childhood and ruined my chances at a healthy relationship, is actually a saint.

 My sister called some days after I had made my decision, and we spoke about our father's death, deciding it was for the best. His mental illness had made his life difficult, disconnected, and complete chaos. A thought crossed my mind that I had not considered before this phone call and I asked my sister, "Do you think Dad was liberated; do you think the stairs in Goindwal actually worked?"

My sister was speaking to me from Salt Lake City, Utah, where we grew up. It was dark there and she was getting ready for work in the early morning hours. Within moments of asking this, a little sparrow came up to her window, popping back and forth along the sill. My sister immediately switched the call over to FaceTime on her smartphone so I could visualize the little bird that looked black in the shadow of the darkness over the camera. I immediately recognized the significance and we both said, "Hi Dad!" We cried together — my question was answered immediately. This is the power of alchemy. This is God.

DO WE CHOOSE OUR PARENTS?

I believe we choose our parents. At least this makes me feel better and it makes a lot of sense that we may pick the people and environments that will help us grow within a particular lifetime. It also feels accurate that some souls choose specific missions to help larger groups of people heal. I believe that people play certain roles in our life that are predestined, and maybe even karmic. Sometimes these roles do not necessarily feel good, but they help us change.

It feels like I chose my parents. I can imagine myself now, looking down from Heaven watching my mother and father meet for the first time. My father took my mother on a motorcycle ride on their first date. He was high on drugs. The motorcycle crashed and they ended up in the emergency room of the hospital where they called their parents — my grandparents — and asked for help. This just so happened to be the same hospital I was born at. Those grandparents ended up helping to raise me, when it was difficult for my parents as a result of their unhealed original wounds. I must have looked down from Heaven and said, "Look over there: yes, right there, they are perfect."

Whether it is healthy or not, women date men because they see themselves and their past within the man in front of them. Men date women for the same reason. Both feel a familiar essence from their own parents, and witness unhealed — and often unknown — parts of themselves. Relationships are one of the best mirrors to visualize our wounds from childhood. Changing these patterns is difficult, but possible. These original wounds create the template for our life and are often based on conditional love or trauma. As we grow older, we will repeat them. The healing of these wounds is the healing of generations of people who were not connected to Source and disconnected from the heart. It is by far the greatest act of service on the planet to take on the healing of these wounds. Alchemists carry a heavy load.

We all face patterns — or templates — within our family systems, which are then experienced within ourselves and exposed through our relationships. These may include unavailability to love or connect, unworthiness, lack, attachment, and ignorance. I am not encouraging you to go to therapy to speak about these issues and recreate the experience. I am not suggesting that you get angry with your family or parents. It is probably not the best idea to leave your partner. It is also not in your best interest to focus on the drama and trauma. What I do want you to do is become aware of your original wounds from childhood, identify where the patterns have been repeated in your relationships, and begin the change today.

To do this, you must remain open-minded and understand that on one level all of this is happening. Your trauma, self-doubt, pain, and fate are all living out within an experience that you call life. On another level of reality, it is not. These are two different vibrational narratives to choose from. It is possible to jump timelines or accelerate through your past by creating a new life narrative. Your narrative is your narrative until you decide that you want to change it. When you decide to change the template, to acknowledge and release your original wounds, you leave the old you behind. You essentially die and resurrect into a new life.

IDENTIFYING FAMILY TEMPLATES

Templates provide the blueprint for the general structure of a system. This book will help you to see that it is possible to break down wounded templates of what a woman, mother, family, and relationship look like so that you can create a new template for your life. This can be done within the relationship you are in now or through a new one. When you choose to live a new narrative, the world around you will respond to this choice. The majority of this book will discuss how to create a new template for a conscious relationship, and ultimately the family unit. Before I discuss this, it is necessary for you to become aware of your original wounds and identify how these old patterns are playing out in your life.

Life is a hologram, similar to a video game. The game world you are playing in is an experience of your subconscious, or experiences from the past, that live within your underworld. In this game, either you get played or you become the player. Everyone in your life is acting as a mirror to your internal world, representing feelings, circumstances, and people from your personal past or family history. You are not awake until you begin to identify these patterns, heal, and actively choose not to repeat them.

If you create self-love internally, you will simultaneously experience this externally, enabling you to navigate situations and avoid people who do not mirror this reality back to you. On the other hand, if you were programmed with low self-confidence and lack of love, your current life will mirror this back to you through your interactions with others. Understanding that your present circumstances expose ancient parts of yourself is a form of self-psychology and a necessary step in healing. Here are a few wounded family templates that may be familiar to you because they are playing out in your current relationships.

Wounded Family Templates

- If you had an unavailable father or mother figure who was mentally, physically, and emotionally not there to meet your needs, or who could not provide the security and love you needed to thrive, you may find yourself clinging and attaching to any person that has a similar vibration later in life. That person can make you become insecure and anxious when they cannot provide you the love you desire. You always wanted this love from your parents, so you will play out this same scenario in your relationships until the original wound is healed.

- If you experienced any form of mental illness in parental figures growing up, this may cause you to attract partners to your life that need mental, physical or emotional healing. As you try to heal your partner, you will ultimately be attempting to heal your original wound, or the mental illness you grew up with.

- If a father or mother figure emotionally or physically abused you in childhood, getting hurt is normal for you. You don't know what it is like to be uplifted or feel good about yourself, so you seek partners that provide the same vibration as your original template. You continually pick partners or friends that put you down mentally or physically — in subtle or obvious ways — because you do not know any better.

- If in childhood you were enmeshed with your parental figure and there were no boundaries, you may have become their life partner because they didn't have a partner themselves. When this happens, it is not uncommon to avoid love or partnership because of the programming that love is all-encompassing or need-based. You may also lack boundaries in relationships later in life.

If your internal world is full of fear, negativity, and painful memories of the past, you will recreate your reality from this vibration. Your relationships and external environments will always reflect the areas that you need to work on. When you heal, you will internally navigate life from a place of love and move into your destiny of serving others. The only way to experience true happiness is through your internal landscape. If you rely on the external world or other people to make you happy, you will feel out of control. Our planet is changing at a rapid pace and we can no longer rely on external environments for security. The individuals that will thrive in this new world are the ones that are navigating their reality from the inside and not relying on anything from the outside for their happiness.

THE ORIGINAL WOUNDS WITHIN YOUR RELATIONSHIPS

If you are feeling pain, or repeating neurotic thoughts in your mind based on your past, or you are worried about the future, you are losing energy. Once you identify your original wounds, you can then identify how they play out within the relationships in your life. As you now know, you are a hologram of your past playing out in the present. You are repeating your wounds or trauma from childhood with new actors. This template was also played out by many generations in your family. If you do some research, you will likely find a common thread to your original wound that goes back many generations.

I work with clients globally to help them identify their templates and original wounds, applying the content of my previous books, my clinical knowledge, and an understanding of meditation to their lives. One client I was working with explained that her husband would not show an emotional response when she cried about a recent death and that this was ruining her marriage. She felt that he could not handle her emotions and that he had abandoned her. I could see clearly that this was the main pattern of her childhood. When she cried as a child, her mother pretended that she did not exist. I asked her when her mother had been emotionally abandoned in her own life, so we could locate that original wound that was being passed down through the generations. My client explained that her mother's mother died when she was a child. She had always been told of a memory of her mother crying over the coffin at the funeral, yet could not remember emotion from her mother as she grew up. Her mother had become emotionally unavailable as a result of her own pain. I asked my client if her husband was always emotionally unavailable and she said that no, he was not.

The recent death my client had experienced catalyzed her original wound to arise for healing for herself and generations back. Her husband was playing the role of her mother during their current fights. She recognized that once she healed the wound around her mother's emotional abandonment, he would no longer need to play this role for her to help open her heart. The healing had to be done within and she could not blame him for being this way until she was healed internally. I provided her a completely new outlook on her relationship. My client recognized that she had to heal her original wounds around her mother in order to save her marriage.

An original wound or template creates a vibration or frequency. It keeps you in the lower three chakras (or energy centers) — the first chakra: safety and fear or the father wound, the second chakra: sexual-based trauma or the mother wound, the third chakra: personal power and self-esteem. Changing your vibration is not easy as it means you have to move into love or a higher center — the heart chakra. The vibration emitted from the original wounds within you will attract other people with the same vibration or wounds, which will either help to heal yours or perpetuate the problem. What happens within the relationship depends on your level of awareness and how you navigate the narrative.

Once a couple's contract of marriage is made, it isn't uncommon that their original wounds will be played out. At the beginning of the relationship, the patterns may not be apparent, but over time you will love the other person the only way you were shown love. You will play out the patterns your parents played around you, especially if they were unhealthy. Couples may not even be conscious of the fact that they are each reflecting the other person's wounds. They just know that they don't feel happy or "in love" with each other anymore.

When I asked my client to reflect upon her husband's wound, we could see that she was playing the role of her husband's ex-wife who had deeply hurt him. When my client became emotionally unavailable, he was reacting from the original wound that was played out throughout his life, which was the belief that women are emotionally unbalanced and out of control. This likely came from his mother and was reflected through his marriages. I showed her that when they fought, they were fighting from the place of the wound and regressing back to the age that the pain occurred (a concept I will discuss later in the book). When she recognized that they were both just playing the roles of their parents, her entire outlook on the marriage shifted from a place of blame to one of changing internally.

If you are not in a vibration of love, and your heart is not healed, you will pick partners that are complementary to your original wounds. Most people essentially marry their parents or caregivers because this is what is familiar to them. No relationship is one-sided, and you cannot project that the problems are within your partner. The problem is within you and your programmed understanding of what a relationship looks like. If you were never taught security, love, patience, and proper communication, you will have to learn this on your own through the expansion of new experiences.

Begin to honor the people that are playing in your programmed reality, or hologram. Have some pity and compassion for them. They are only there to help you see hidden parts of yourself. Since the original wound carries a lower vibration, healing it means that you have to change yours. This isn't easy — it requires courage and dedicated work on yourself. There are negative forces here on Earth that do not want you to succeed. These forces want to keep you in the same vibration and locked within your mind. The path of liberation is through the heart, and this is where I will lead you.

I want you to succeed, and I believe that you will, through alchemical transformation. I don't want you to continue identifying with your trauma or playing out the same patterns from childhood. My goal is for you to begin to identify your wounds and not identify as your wounds. It is necessary to acknowledge how powerful you are and just how much you can sabotage your own life. Throughout this book I will continue to discuss my original wound, how it related to my father, the subsequent men I attracted, and my personal journey through alchemy to heal. Through this story of the hero's journey, I hope to show you how family templates repeat throughout life, and that you can consciously heal your past patterns to create from the present moment, which is based on love, rather than create reality from the past which has conditions on it.

Your original wounds will not be the same as mine. They may be from a different caregiver and a different sex. You may identify many patterns and even require a counselor to help you remember. Once you do though, you will start your alchemical transformation which will lead to the healing of your heart. Below are some questions and ideas for you to explore. They will be expanded upon as you move through the book.

1. Identify your original wounds. What painful moments from your past hold you back from accomplishing all that you came here to do? Was this wound a result of one specific parent or caregiver? What were the general behaviors

or belief systems that you were programmed with as a result? You will most likely be able to remember specific moments in your life that were quite painful. It is important to note what your age was in these memories, because your personality likely regresses to this age in similar situations in present time.

2. When you notice yourself reacting in your relationships, ask yourself what age you are reacting from. How old were you when you first felt this way? As wounds are triggered, we usually respond to the other person as if we are the same age as when the wound happened because ultimately, we have not grown up yet.

3. Note how these ingrained patterns and belief systems arise within your current relationship. This relationship can be with the opposite sex or the same sex. This book is focused on romantic relationships, because this is where the wounds are usually amplified, but you may be able to see your wounds play out within friendships and at work too.

4. Notice how the dynamics are the same as your childhood — just with new people. Describe specific situations that have recently happened within your relationships and note if you experienced a similar scenario in your childhood. You may only be able to see the pattern by feeling the

emotions around it that represent the emotions you felt growing up.

5. Identify how many relationships you have been in that have played out these same patterns.

6. Promise yourself that today you will begin to raise your vibration, change the subconscious patterns, and stop repeating the wound.

7. You will continue to get retriggered by the wound over and over again, even as you heal. This will happen through the same person or new ones. Healing is the path of noticing that the other person is mirroring a part of you that needs help. Do not get angry at these individuals. They are angels sent in disguise to make sure that you are living up to your promise and are willing to raise your worth and love yourself more. On the hero's journey, these people will help you to navigate human character and integrity.

8. Through this self-psychology, you will begin to notice the ways that you self-sabotage your own success and relationships. When you interact in drama and trauma, and do not learn to consciously walk away from the situation that represents an old pattern, you are sabotaging. Identifying the self-sabotaging personalities that live within you will help you to see where

you do not love yourself enough to raise your worth and find self-sovereignty.

9. Healing the original wounds, the wounded children within you, and the personal ways you destroy your success isn't necessarily a pleasant process.

You must first acknowledge where the pain originated from to let it go. Essentially, you have to find the root of the issue and where the original belief system came from. Sometimes these belief systems of unworthiness are so ancient you cannot tell where you end and they begin. I can promise you that if you are on the path to healing, these patterns will be reflected through your environment and relationships.

Each time you feel irritated, upset, emotionally absent or hurt by another, you are essentially feeling a part of you that has been left unhealed; otherwise you would not have a big reaction to the experience. The feelings of jealousy, avoidance, attachment, anger, greed, shame, or judgement are not caused by the person that you are projecting them on. These emotions exist within you first or you wouldn't be able to experience them.

When you are healed and recognize these emotions within yourself or another, there is little to no reaction. You will just observe that it is happening. This quality of presence creates a sense of compassion and neutrality, making it easy to move on from anything that takes you out of balance or hooks you back into old patterns of negativity.

If you are wondering why your relationship is not working or why every partner you meet does not essentially meet your needs, it is because you have not created a relationship with yourself. If you are looking for a relationship to heal you or meet your needs, you will only find this lack within other people reflected back to you. Each person's connection to him — or herself determines the level of connection to another. To heal, you must grow up. Alchemy can significantly speed up this process so that you can live your best life.

ALCHEMY: THE STEPS TO HEALING

Alchemy is a spiritual technology that was brought to the planet through the Emerald Tablet. Alchemists named the stages of the alchemical process, taken from the Emerald Tablet, as **The Great Work**, and created a formula that consists of seven operations (with a hidden eighth operation) to help spiritual warriors navigate the process of awakening. Each of the next seven chapters of *Alchemy of Becoming* is devoted to one of these stages. They are an intrinsic part of healing our original wounds and helping humanity move into the heart center.

According to Dennis Hauck, author of *The Emerald Tablet: Alchemy for Personal Transformation*, this tablet was first introduced to the planet in ancient Egypt by the god Thoth (who was later known as Hermes Trismegistus). Thoth was the transcriber of ancient Egyptian texts, transferring the word of God into an energetic transmission. He established a spiritual technology and tool for transformation on Earth for each human to utilize when their soul was ready. Everyone is consistently going through the alchemical process, but most are not aware of it and do not make it to the last steps. As we move into this next Golden Age, more initiates will enter all of the stages of transformation and be ready to open their hearts. As this happens, the technology of the Emerald Tablet will be reignited on Earth and alchemical transformation will become more common.

Alchemy is an ancient process of initiation that transforms the soul within the earthly body so that the human becomes a Divine Co-creator with God. This process is incredibly strenuous to the mental, physical, and emotional bodies as changes occur both internally and externally. It has been often sensationalized in modern media and on design platforms, but is not fully comprehensible through these depictions. Alchemy is not a brand name or social media hashtag. Nor is the process solely carried out in a laboratory, though this is how it was kept hidden and documented throughout history.

Alchemy is a gift that helps you to awaken by transforming your consciousness to match the Universe. If the alchemy of the physical world were to be completed in a lab, as it has been done for thousands of years, the scientist would break down metals in a beaker, or glass container, with the ultimate purpose of creating gold. For spiritual purposes, your body is the beaker and your soul surrenders to the purification process. The secret of this spiritual technology is that it can only be done within the human body. This alchemical transformation helps you to find the gold within through love. An initiate must essentially allow the elements — fire, earth, air, water, and ether — to radically change them, and understand that The Great Work is done simultaneously on Earth and within higher dimensional fields.

CHAPTER TWO: CALCINATION

STEP INTO THE FIRE

The first stage of transformation is Calcination, which is essentially what happens when fire burns away the egocentric parts of the personality. This period creates the death of the ego and destroys parts of the human personality that are attached to the material world. The more an individual, or even a society at large, is connected to the illusions of the material realm, the greater the burn. Life will essentially be turned upside down and transformed into utter chaos so that the deep-rooted attachments that prevent an individual from looking inside to their original source can be destroyed.

Calcination is represented by blackness or a period of darkness that the spiritual warrior must enter. It is a chemical process where the lower functioning thoughts and defense mechanisms of the persona are identified and the process of their destruction begins. Dennis Hauck explains that under normal circumstances, Calcination occurs during a person's life in small stages or through various bothersome issues that are resolved. These gradual assaults and obstacles are natural. However, when an initiate on the spiritual path enters the Calcination phase, the assault by fire is not gradual. The darkness is pitch black.

When the coronavirus hit the planet in 2020, the world began to globally go through Calcination and The Great Work together. The virus created an international shutdown of business and commerce, forcing individuals to retreat into their homes and let go of the outside world as they knew it. This shelter-in-place initiative spread across the planet. When life forces us to change our routine, we lose our sense of control and are forced to question what we require to live and what is necessary to survive. When the inhabitants of our world were taken out of their normal routines, the subconscious of each individual was pressurized, allowing all of the obsessive thoughts or feelings that were once easily avoided through activity to arise.

This global shutdown provided an exceptional example of the power of Calcination. When you are forced to stop and take a look at yourself because of a catastrophic life event, you can more easily identify the things you are attached to. You would have likely been ignorant, or lacked awareness, around these issues before being forced into a phase where what you deem to be important is taken away. Calcination essentially burns away the suffering that can be experienced through the energies created in the three lower chakras. These include, as mentioned earlier, issues around safety, fear of death, attachment to material possessions, sexual desires or dysfunctions, power, money, and survival. In order to move from lower vibrational issues into the heart center and beyond, these conditions must be confronted and healed.

Certainty creates a false sense of safety. Stagnancy creates sloth or sluggishness. Most people pick certainty over changing and remain in the same unhealthy situations throughout their lives without choosing to take a conscious look at their circumstances. Alchemy is not stagnant. Alchemists move through the fires of change until unpredictability and chaos in the outside world do not affect the calmness in their internal world. As you go through your alchemical journey, it is normal to be terrified of the unknown. There is a leap in consciousness that must happen when you stop settling and you get sick of your own suffering and pain. Once you are willing to break the pattern, or let go of the human story of suffering, life changes and you create a new narrative.

When you experience the incredible power of fire — and you don't actually die — you learn that there is really nothing to fear. During Calcination, the element fire consumes every part of your identity and your perception of reality. At points, it can be so intense that it is common to feel that life is not worth living or that you could physically leave this Earth, but in most cases, you don't. Calcination is an essential step to conquering deep fears. You will experience a death of the personality or ego, which is the projection or image that your human self gives the world — which is not an accurate representation of the soul.

Letting go of the false parts of yourself projected to the world, and the attachments that feed this image, is the ultimate spiritual death. Once you face your greatest internal nightmares (and they are just that — internal), not much in the external world can threaten you because you have essentially lost it all already. Alchemy prepares you for physical death by helping you to experience it before you leave your body. Letting go of the need to control is an essential step in the journey.

A STORY OF CALCINATION

Part of the letting go process of the Calcination stage of awakening is understanding that something bigger than you is in charge of your life and you have control over nothing but your reactions. A great amount of force is often needed to create these changes. What might feel like an absolute combustion, is actually a controlled burn from God that forces you to adjust to a new way of being in the world. This will help to release all of the heavy mental constructs and belief systems to get your

CHAPTER TWO: CALCINATION 57

soul on the path to finding its true essence. Here is my story of surrender to the fire of transformation.

I have experienced several Calcination experiences in my life, but looking back I can see that these little fires were just preparing me for the catastrophic burn that the Heavens would eventually send. My first experience of the fire element was my spontaneous Kundalini opening in 2012; I discussed this in my first two books. As energy ascended from the base of my spine up through each of the chakras and out the top of my head, my life was never the same. I felt as if I had been energetically lit on fire. This fire helped me to burn away my past belief systems. I had to empty, empty, and empty some more. As I let go of my limiting beliefs of what I thought was possible, I began to be led by something greater than me.

Coincidences became more common, passages of books would answer my questions, friends began calling when I thought of their names and my internal patterns in need of healing became very apparent. The Universe led me to individuals and teachers that began to awaken me from the dream I thought was a reality. I discovered that all of my past patterns could be found within me and were outwardly displayed in my relationships. After this experience, my life moved much faster and my consciousness changed at an amplified rate. The changes I was experiencing on the inside began to create outward manifestations that physically moved my life's path forward. My journey began to accelerate even faster after my visit to India to complete the steps of Goindwal. I have already mentioned the significance of my trip to India, but the end of this specific trip is what really changed my life.

A week after completing the stairs of Goindwal, I found myself at the Dalai Lama's Temple in the Himalayan mountains, staying there for a few days. In that early morning of the day of my departure, I was hanging prayer flags in the trees on the circular path that pilgrims walk on within the temple complex. It is common for visitors to hang these prayer flags and make a wish. As I was hanging my flags, I prayed, "Help me to awaken humanity" repeatedly in my head. I do not know why in that moment I chose to say that prayer which I had read in the book *Conversations with God, Book 4* written by Neale Donald Walsch. At the time, I identified saving humanity as a valiant effort to help many, and had no idea that it was really about awakening myself.

Thirty minutes later, before jumping into a cab to head to the airport, I noticed a sequence of oddly shaped photos in various colors of sandstone in my phone. The photos contained a series of designs. One picture clearly depicted an eye shaded in blue and gray, which I realized was the Eye of Horus or the symbol of ancient initiation. I knew that I did not take these pictures because the shapes of the photos ranged from small squares to rectangles and I had never seen this capability on the smartphone I was using. There was no way the pictures could have been taken accidently while the phone was in my bag — and I had not touched it. I counted the photos many times and found forty-six of them. I

CHAPTER TWO: CALCINATION

even showed them to several of my friends for verification and they confirmed what I saw.

The more we let go of our sense of control, the easier it is for us to be led by something greater, which then allows miracles to flow into our life. As an alchemist, you must learn to think outside the box of what is possible. Others may not understand you because they live within the world of logic, but you will be guided to those who do. I could not figure out why I had received forty-six photos or what that number meant. I uploaded the photos onto my computer and there were suddenly forty-eight of them. I recounted each set many times and the numbers were very clear. I was speaking to a friend questioning what the number forty-six meant, when all of a sudden I said out loud, "There are forty-six chromosomes in the DNA." Bingo. But what did the number forty-eight represent?

As an alchemist, you must also develop the ability to listen to a subtle, yet commanding, internal voice that pulls at your heart strings and helps to guide your life. This is the voice of your Higher Self, which is imperceptible to others, but impossible for you to ignore. This voice will tell you where to go and who to avoid if you learn to trust it. I was sitting on my couch in meditation a couple of days later and heard this internal guidance system ask me to take a book off the shelf called *The Ancient Secret of the Flower of Life* by Drunvalo Melchizedek. A friend had given me this book before I moved to Ireland and I had never opened it. I flipped to a page with the title "*The 48 Chromosomes of Christ Consciousness DNA* can be Found in the Great Pyramid." Finding this sentence changed my entire life. The forty-eight chromosomes of Christ Consciousness is the alchemical signature and legacy of love that Jesus left on Earth. For the alchemist, there is a call to action on the hero's journey to begin to live life from the level of the heart. This was my call.

Alchemists have an internal knowing or compass that tells them where they need to go next. By trusting this guidance system, an alchemist can learn to see the unseen and hear the unheard. Silence brings forth salvation. I knew in that instant I would have to make my way to the Great Pyramid and that there was something there that would change my life. I didn't know how I would get inside this sacred site, but I knew I had just "conceived" something that would be birthed in the next nine months.

Within those nine months between the conception of those photos I received and the birth of my new life, I published my first book *Mystical Motherhood* and began to write my second book *Fertile*. The story of how *Fertile* was created is a book in itself. The process of writing it generated a deeper development of my own knowing of where to go in order to receive information from higher dimensions or realities. In his metaphysical books, Carlos Castañeda stated that there are places of power in this world that help us to gain energy, but only a few people know how to find and actually seize these experiences. Alchemists are always hunting for this power.

Power to an alchemist is an energetic transmission that helps the soul to transcend the limitations of the human body. Specific places around the world hold memories which can be easily accessed. When I equated the forty-six photos to DNA, I opened up a new understanding of how to apply the concepts of epigenetics to the period of pregnancy. I was guided to begin to travel to sacred sites along the Rose Ley Line, which are energetic portals to embodying the Divine Feminine and the Holy Grail. I developed an inner knowing as to where to travel to next in Scotland, Ireland, England, France, and beyond, in order to write *Fertile*.

My teacher Celestine Star joined me for part of this pilgrimage. Remember, on the hero's journey there is a call to action and a teacher will commonly step in to help the alchemist in training to cross the threshold and make it to their highest destiny. Celestine flew all the way from the West Coast in America to be with me and one day as we were driving through Scotland, she said to me, "You are about to go through an initiation to learn what the Beloved is. Life as you know it will never be the same and you will be asked to leave. Do you understand what I am saying to you?" When she said this, tears of joy welled in her eyes for me knowing the joy I would eventually experience. No, I did not truly understand the significance of what she said. For some reason I didn't tell her that I was headed to the Great Pyramid in a couple of weeks, but likely she already knew this.

Nine months after receiving the photos in the Himalayas, I found myself in Egypt. A friend had sent me a post on social media regarding a healer named Abdy Electriciteh who was going to Egypt with a group. I had never heard of this man, but I knew I had to go. I believe I spent less than five minutes on his website and then booked the trip without understanding anything about what I was getting myself into. Intuition happens in the first eleven seconds of thought. It is not logical and it happens when you are connected to the One consciousness. Intuition is a trust in a deeper stillness within. When you know, you know. The day I arrived in Egypt I was sitting in this large convention center room with windows facing the Great Pyramid. I had no idea who this man Abdy was, but it appeared that the other ninety people in the room knew him well.

I often regret the words I said at the top of that mountain at the Dalai Lama's Temple. I didn't understand that the awakening of humanity is actually the awakening of each human being from their own illusions, material greed, need to control, and the toxicity of their minds. The journey of awakening humanity is each person's individual journey back to living, without expectations or ego, from the level of their heart. Which is a painful process of letting go of ignorance and attachment.

I soon learned that Abdy is a healer who allows energy from Source to flow through him and transform those in his presence by helping to alter their consciousness and life. The group began to hug one another as a healing energy was emitted from him.

I thought, "What the hell am I doing here? What have I gotten myself into?" Though my logical mind felt discomfort, my soul knew that I was in the right place at the right time. The hugging progressed. It felt odd to hug a group of strangers, but as I continued, I noticed my heart open and that these people were not strangers at all. Each person had a specific, yet familiar, energy. Suddenly, and may I reiterate suddenly, I hugged one man I had never met before in this life, and out of nowhere my entire body lit up energetically. A fire from Heaven began to pour into my body. My subtle body immediately flew up and out and I astral traveled within higher dimensional fields while still remaining stable within the hug on Earth. I began to energetically feel ecstatic and orgasmic love on all levels. I visually experienced myself as pure light.

Let me bring this back to Earth to provide you a new perspective. Places of power remind me of the *Harry Potter* book series. If you have seen the movies, you may remember the train station scene where a door randomly opens and all the Hogwarts students jump through to start their school year. Alchemists are always looking for these doors too. They are the portals that open up dimensions to make the unknown known again. That is what happened on that day in Egypt when I hugged that man. I entered a dimensional doorway and experienced the ancient initiation of what I would later find out is called the Hieros Gamos (at least this is the closest human definition of what I believe may have happened). This is the sacred marriage of the human to the Divine.

The Hieros Gamos is referenced in textbooks as far back as ancient Egypt and Greece and has also been called the Mystic Marriage. This ancient initiation felt like two souls merging in the Higher Realms on all levels or the masculine and feminine becoming One. It activated my internal body and all of the chakra systems. Just like my first glimpse at the element of fire through my Kundalini opening, I was lit on fire for the second time. This time it was not a spark, but a merging with the light and a combustion of the cosmos. My life has never been the same through the power of Calcination. This experience gave me the ability to feel full union with the masculine through a platonic mystical encounter. When I came back to Earth, I realized just how far our fall from grace was and how much healing the masculine and feminine on our planet must go through to feel like One again. This is the story of Adam and Eve leaving Eden.

DARKNESS

In order to experience the light, we have to experience the darkness. Polarities are opposites that can't live without each other. Darkness is essentially just the absence of the light. It is the tunnel that never ends, a locked closet, a cloaked body and the chills of the unknown. It initiates the healing of our deepest wounds and is an essential part of the Calcination stage. After the fire there are always ashes to clean up.

The darkness is frightening, and everyone avoids it because it swallows you up. What individuals don't realize is that it is through the dark that they will reach the light. We intuitively avoid the dark, starting in our childhood. Children always say, "Quick! Turn the light on! I'm scared." Scared of what? is the question. Well, they are fearful of what they cannot see and are unaware of. Our subconscious issues and original wounds are hidden in the murky depths within and always arise in the dark like monsters from our past.

The next day, guided by Abdy, our group received private access to all levels of the Great Pyramid of Giza. I moved from the top chamber of the pyramid down to the lowest chamber and stood within the room where, I had read, that the forty-eight Chromosomes of Christ Consciousness existed within forty-eight encryptions on the walls. After this, our trip continued down the Nile River and we received life-changing energetic experiences in ancient temples of initiation that are impossible to put into words. And it was during this week that I made the biggest decision of my life — I decided to leave my marriage and life as I knew it.

I have lived in a new house every two years my entire life and have never fully identified one place as home. It was written in our wedding vows that home is where the heart is and I took that quite literally. When I decided to leave, I didn't know where to move to because I was living in Ireland. I did not want to return to the life my husband and I had created with his family or where I grew up. The man I hugged in that conference center room lived in New York, and over and over, I kept hearing the words: "Move to Brooklyn; you will find a temple and you will heal." Just as I had followed the sentence in that book that led me to the Great Pyramid, I followed this simple direction and the energy that had been created in my heart through this most recent mystical experience. I knew surely and deeply that I needed to move to Brooklyn with my children and ask my soon-to-be ex-husband to follow us, despite the fact that I had never been there before.

I met my husband at the age of eighteen on the first day of college and we had been together for approximately seventeen years. I only knew life with this man. This book will not include a single detail of the real reasons why I left or the pain of the cover-up that occurred after I did (even though this story would make a great movie and a much better book plotline). It will also not include any details of our beautiful marriage and the absolute love I have for this man that brings me to tears as I write this. What I will include is that sometimes our closest loved ones play the role of breaking our heart. They are not the actual cause of our heartbreak, as this pain is hidden in the darkness of our past — they just sacrifice themselves for our growth and play as an actor to remind us of our original wounds.

No one really knows the truth about most people's lives because the truth is hard to see. It is difficult to swallow because it is so transparent and real. Most people prefer to live in ignorance and not know what is hidden under the covers, within the walls of the house you thought was so sturdy, or under the clothes of real vulnerability. Truth destroys ignorance and shakes the very foundation that you had once based your life upon. No one likes to be this open, this real or this expansive.

Alchemists live entirely differently though. When they jump off a cliff, they do so without a landing plan because the alchemist knows that the only one in control is God. The sheer velocity of their actions puts many things in perspective for countless people and generations, even though it may take years to see the veracity in their decision-making. I always jump, knowing that something greater will catch me.

The day I got back from Egypt, and the moment I walked in the door of our home in Ireland, I walked up to my husband and told him I was leaving him. It was the first time in my life I had the energy and boldness to do this. The fire of Calcination was still running through my bones. He did not try to stop me. He just moved on with his own life. Our separation process had started on an energetic level before this through an omen. Alchemists are guided by omens, which are messages from God that appear through people, dreams, symbols, animals or prophetic events.

Before my trip to Egypt, we had gone as a family back to California; he and I were taking one last walk together along a reservoir before our departure. I was walking ahead of him, and he called, and said, "I can't move forward: there is a huge rattlesnake hissing at me." This had never happened on a walk before. And I had walked past this rattlesnake, but did not see it. He said that once I had stepped over the serpent, it curled up and began to hiss at him. I could hear the rattlesnake, but did not understand what he was talking about. I told him, "I don't see the snake, just cross over it or go around it and come this direction with me."

I didn't turn around and go back in his direction because I would have been taking the long way home. He said, "How can you not see it? It is right there! There is no way I can get past." I honestly could not see it and did not feel any fear. If he did not come with me, he would have to turn around and walk backwards many miles and we would need to find a place to meet in the middle where the two roads merged, which was out of our way. He said, "No. I'll meet you somewhere in the *middle* or I will *eventually* make it home." He turned around and walked away and I walked alone in the other direction and headed directly home.

The snake is often depicted as the ouroboros, or snake eating its own tail in renewal of life. In the story of Adam and Eve, in Genesis in the Bible, a serpent approached Eve and told her to eat fruit from the tree in the *middle* of the garden — the one tree that God had told the couple not to eat from. Eve was like the ouroboros snake. Before she ate this fruit, she was at One with God and happily living with Adam. The story goes that evil entered this world when Eve made the mistake of eating the fruit. This narrative made the principle of woman the principle of all evil. This story is very outdated, don't you think? Imagine what would have happened if Eve had never seen that snake? Eve's desire to eat the fruit with Adam led to the archetypal story of our fall from grace into duality and our experience of polarity. This merging back into Oneness that this book is about is our way back home to God. That is the type of story I am telling here.

After deciding to leave my marriage, I fell into the deepest and darkest depression of my life; I did not rise out of it for almost two years. When I decided to leave my husband, I did not seek legal counsel, think through how I would move out of Ireland and back into the United States or consider the lifetime consequences. I did not take years planning my departure or consider how I would financially survive. I did not think about how I would take care of a three- and four-year-old with little help or what life as a single mother would be like.

I was absolutely unaware of the amount of pain, discomfort, grief, and isolation I was about to experience. These emotions were already a part of my marriage, and they shortly became fully exposed. I walked into the unknown just like one would walk off a plank on a ship or jump off a bridge. There was no going back, and I only knew to follow my internal voice that had never led me wrong. I walked out on safety, wealth, security, and illusion to live my truth. I chose to move to a city that no single mother would dare to face alone — New York City. I did this all because the strings of my heart were yanking me there and I had to find that temple I was told I would heal within. Alchemists always follow their heart's guidance system.

In the darkness, you are forced to face yourself and cannot accurately see where you are going next. It is only you leading you, hoping to find that light. The inability to know the future brings up your need to control and to know what is going to happen next in order to feel safe. Darkness doesn't allow that level of security. It is not purposely trying to hurt you — it is just being itself, which is an all-encompassing dark matter that holds you and all of your absurd emotions within it. Once you relax into the darkness that takes over your life during the phase of Calcination, a great amount of peace is allowed to enter. Then eventually, something magical begins to happen. You begin to gain trust ... but first you must face your absolute worst fears.

FEAR

When you follow the voice inside, you lose your sense of self. In my world, I can't do anything wrong. There's no plan. I am just an internal yes. That voice is clear to you, it's clear to all of us, but it's overlaid by the thoughts we believe. I used to call it the voice of the heart. I didn't have a teacher to tell me, "This is spiritual and this isn't," so I just kept following the voice and losing everything. People would say, "You're crazy," and I would just say, "Oh," and keep on following the voice. — **Byron Katie**

CHAPTER TWO: CALCINATION

The life I thought I would live until my death was over in a blink of an eye, and I just kept listening to that little voice inside me that was navigating my life. As my human Self began to die, I allowed my Divine Self to take over. A lot of fear arises as you let go and trust that God has a better plan for you. Though it may sound crazy, that little voice said, "Move to Brooklyn and you will find a temple." I had never been to Brooklyn and I highly doubted that there were any temples there, but the voice had never led me wrong.

Fear is heavy and depressive. It is a long, dark corridor and the imagined enemy is hiding in the shadows. Fear is the pain of the past and the not knowing what the future will bring. In order to rise above the feeling of fear, you must rise above all of the darkness that is within you and all of the parts that think you cannot make it. The transition from being in relationship for most of one's life to being single is one of the most powerful and painful places to be in because you must let go of your identity. While it is common for men to maintain their identity through their career, it is just as common for women to maintain their identity through a relationship. I only knew myself in relation to my husband. Being alone was foreign to me.

Losing your identity, or who you thought you were in human form, is the beginning of the loss of ego. For most people, the space of being alone is too much. The pain is unbearable. If we try to escape from this pain by quickly entering another relationship, numbing out on drugs or alcohol or becoming busy with work, we don't get to learn what the relationship taught us. There is no time for self-reflection. When we are forced to come face-to-face with our "aloneness," we learn to meet our needs by ourselves. The dark space in between helps us to learn how to bring a whole human being into our next relationship.

I took a flight from Dublin to New York City to find an apartment a couple of weeks after I told my husband that I wanted to end our marriage. My children stayed home with their father and our nanny. He would also soon take this flight to find his apartment close to us as we all left our old lives behind to create a new one. I saw one apartment online that looked quite lovely. When I arrived, I found it was not in an actual apartment building — it was in a church that had been developed into one.

The church had been fully restored into a 12-unit complex. All of the original intricately designed encryptions on the exterior large-paneled doors, stained glass windows and original wood had been salvaged and used to maintain its unique architectural style. When I stood at the entrance of what was once the abbey of the church where the priests lived, I saw a very large dove intricately designed in colored glass. This dove just so happened to be on the outside of the unit I was going to live in. I noticed that the church was built in 1888 and that the symbol of the Cathars (an equilateral cross) and the Sphinx was on the outside. The apartment was the first and only one I viewed upon arriving in Brooklyn. I have been told renting the first apartment you see is incredibly uncommon, if not impossible, in the New York real estate market.

The Universe speaks in symbols and when they open for you, it is similar to receiving a cosmic library of information. Another way for an alchemist to understand symbols is to consider them like applications downloaded on a smartphone. When you open an application, you discover a world of information within that may teach you something new. I knew immediately that this was where I was supposed to move because the symbols began to speak to me. The dove was the symbol of the book I was writing at the time — *Fertile*. The Cathars symbol represents the Holy Grail and the line of protectors of Mary Magdalene. The forty-eight encryptions I had set out to find in Egypt are in an underground tunnel in the lower chamber of the Great Pyramid that connects to the Sphinx. The numbers 888 represent the Goddess Isis and Jesus or the Holy Child. The number 8 is also the number of the alchemist. I just so happened to be moving into apartment 8 in a church built in 1888.

These symbols are also found along the Rose Ley Line in Europe and in all of the specific places I had traveled to before visiting the Great Pyramid. The church was located on Adelphi Street in Brooklyn and was originally called the Church of St. Michael. There is a large statue of St. Michael in Magdalene's cave in the South of France, which is where I started writing and researching *Fertile*. When I asked the locals why, I was told it is because he is the archangel who is the protector of the Divine Feminine on Earth. One day, months after moving into this apartment, a friend said, "Do you realize that you live on Adelphi Street and that the Temple of Delphi was one of the original sacred birthing temples in ancient Greece where the women would connect to higher power to bring down holy souls?" And you know, I had not even thought of that.

It turns out that the symbol of the dove is also connected to the ancient birthing priestesses of Delphi. I like surprises like this. I enjoy experiencing omens that appear in my life to guide me. I appreciate being in the right place at the right time. I honor places of power and I know I could not have written *Fertile* or *Alchemy of Becoming* in any other location. I appreciate the language of the Universe and the way it talks to me. I enjoy following my heart and finding the jewels that the logical mind discovers later which make up the puzzle pieces of life while on the path of destiny. The Universe was not joking when it told me to leave my life, move to Brooklyn, and find a temple. Even in the midst of great fear during the Calcination stage of alchemy, incredible miracles can occur.

CHAPTER THREE: DISSOLUTION

OPENING THE FLOODGATES

Heart-opening on the level of humanity is coinciding with heart-opening on the level of the individual. For the heart to be opened, one has to go through whatever energies the heart has been holding and hindering its opening. That means the energies of sadness, grief, heartbreak and so forth, have to be released. Releasing such energies means having a real experience creating the emotions. Heart-opening happens in stages. When you go through those emotions you end up with euphoria and experiencing your being through your heart. Then, any time you are at your high vibration, you will be in a heart space. Anytime you are in your low vibration, you will be in head space. This can alternate as many as a few times a day. It's exhausting for the emotional body and confusing for the mind, to the extent that some people experience bipolar thoughts and depression. — **Abdy Electriciteh**

Feelings are meant to be felt, yet most of us don't know how to be with our emotions in a balanced and neutral way. When you begin to unravel the decades of distortion, you will notice how far away you are from mental balance, clarity, and love. The period of Dissolution during the awakening process reveals the individual's soul. It exposes all the lessons that the soul must go through to essentially dissolve. Issues around control, letting go, breaking habits, and feeling deeply arise during this time. This is a period where your absolute deepest pains and worst imagined fears rise to the surface to be recollected and worked through. During this stage, the alchemist will take time for inner reflection.

Individuals typically project all of their issues onto someone else, blaming another for their inability to be happy. Grief arises in great intensity as the person recognizes that it is the broken fragments of their past and inability to respond from their heart that create pain in the present. All of the rejected and unprocessed parts of the mind must be observed. Withdrawing psychological projections and judgements is a very difficult habit to break. The individual has to stop blaming their problems on another and begin to take responsibility for what they create in their life. This is a necessary step to clean out the alchemist's mind so he or she can create from a place of love rather than a place of fear. When this shift is created, there is a new flow of energy within the individual, put forth for something greater than the promotion of neurotic human tendencies.

CHAPTER THREE: DISSOLUTION

I didn't know what to expect once I fully moved into my new apartment with my kids in New York. I started to date immediately, hoping to fill the vast emptiness inside. I dated the man I had met in the conference room in Egypt and it fell apart as fast as it started. I thought I found love, many times. I had an overwhelming, obsessive-compulsive, and chaotic feeling towards men after leaving my husband. This is normal, right? This is what I knew as love, because when I was younger, that is how I attempted to get attention from my parents. The chaos of my childhood, and the mental illness my father experienced were reflected through almost every relationship I had with every man in my life. I was terrified to be alone, but it was through the aloneness I found myself.

Chaotic and broken minds were normal for me, and because I felt the urge to heal them, I attracted men that mirrored that reality. I was recreating my original wound over and over again, hoping to find love through the cracks of my pain. This was my base frequency — a pattern so ingrained within me that I was not aware that it was happening until the alchemical phase of Dissolution. The moment I became conscious of the fact that I was not loved in the way I had always desired, and that I had deeply disrespected myself within these relationships — that moment felt like a sledge hammer hitting a mirror and shattering it into thousands of pieces.

An alchemist, like a painter creating art on a canvas, eventually learns through trial and error that they create their reality. This realization is destabilizing and shocking. As your heart opens, you will likely recreate your original pain, and until your pain is healed, you are essentially controlled by it. This mind control is mental slavery and it not only affects you on a personal level, but can captivate you on a group level too. Unhealed group pain can control the masses. This is seen through the media, social movements (that often camouflage themselves through positivity), wars, and genocide. The key is recognizing that it is happening and not get hooked by the mind control.

After the divorce, the amount of grief that poured through me was unfathomable. It felt like I was experiencing my own pain along with the grief of everyone around me. I could not delineate where I started and someone else physically or energetically began. I experienced an extreme form of depression and mental breakdown where my old Self died with the destruction of my inner and outer worlds. Nothing made sense in my life — and this period was necessary to eventually experience peace. This period is typically called a "Dark Night of the Soul" in spiritual teachings. I was in such a deep trance that I would often find myself riding the subway in the wrong direction upwards to one hour with tears welling up in my eyes.

During this period, I dissolved all of my attachments to the outward world and this helped me to develop my self-sovereignty and emancipate me from my own mental slavery. I had been used to a refined life with exceptional resources and wealth. Walking away showed me just how much

CHAPTER THREE: DISSOLUTION

these material resources had become my identity, my thoughts, and projections of reality. I was programmed that safety came from secure finances and I equated this to love. You may experience the opposite and face great financial difficulty. Excessive forms of wealth and lack of money often equate to the same vibration — the feeling of scarcity.

In order to move my energy into my heart, I had to work through all of my lower chakra issues around material wealth, loss of power, sexuality, fear, and control. These larger concepts began to be mirrored to me through interactions in my relationships. On top of coming to terms with losing my identity with these outside resources, it was at this time that, after thirty-five years of suffering, I finally learned that my father's absence was keeping me out of my heart center. Your original wound may not be from your father and may be a result of other memories with different individuals. Your original wound may be associated with the color of your skin, your cultural identity, the rape you experienced, the death of a loved one or overall trauma. The key is recognizing that if your mind is experiencing projected painful thoughts, you are recreating that in the environment around you and thus your heart cannot be fully felt.

TRAUMA BONDING IN RELATIONSHIPS

Traumatic experiences leave traces within our bodies. They occupy space within our cells, DNA, bones, and organs. Trauma can be simply defined as anything disruptive we experienced in our mother's womb or in childhood that didn't get a resolution. Without healing, we continually call in situations throughout our lives to work through the trauma and programming we received. Everyone is looking for a resolution so that they can live a more fulfilled life, but the alchemist makes it his or her mission to identify and dissolve the past to create a better future.

The alchemist not only clears their own personal trauma, but tends to take on the trauma of a family line, community, or humanity at large. Patterns play out within the alchemist's life that are much larger than just their own. In the process of energetically releasing the trauma within themselves, they allow others to do the same. When the alchemist faces their biggest demons, like magic they hold this ability within their field or aura. The healed wound is broadcasted from their energy body and can be actively or passively transferred to individuals that are also ready to heal. When an alchemist moves into their heart center, many people follow, because the vibration of the heart affects the surrounding environment with great intensity.

It takes a tremendous amount of effort to be a highly functioning human being when you are filled with pain from the past. Trauma is a form of mind control that affects us personally, culturally, and globally. We cannot envision a new future for our planet if we are stuck in our past. There is no way to create what we came here to do fully without the release of these ancient patterns. Change comes as the person gathers him or herself back together by healing different aspects of themselves to create more self-love, sovereignty, grace, peace, and sobriety. Your soul's mission is linked to a combination of what makes you feel enthusiastic and what you have alchemized and healed within. Without healing, we lack worthiness, self-love, boundaries, clarity, and even purpose. I want you to become so strong that you are unexploitable.

Our trauma, if left unhealed, will dictate our life. It becomes the ghost that haunts us, constantly lurking in our field. Until we become aware of the experiences or memories, we repeatedly replay scenes without knowing we are doing so. The pain is buried in our subconscious or unconscious mind, like trash in a garbage can that hasn't been taken out. Trauma is registered and programmed within every individual differently. Trauma causes actual changes in the brain which affect us mentally. Repeating the patterns from your childhood as an adult is not necessarily from lack of willpower or bad choices. You are just running on the same neuron pattern from when the trauma was first created.

From a spiritual perspective, trauma causes the person to energetically explode in extreme conditions. As the event occurs, parts of the energy body of the individual split off like shards of broken glass to protect themselves. They remain isolated — traumatized, separated. The person is essentially not energetically whole until they heal. The traumatized parts of their soul can only return when it is safe to do so. We know that the physical body shows scarring, and negative programming is similarly evident in the emotional body. A traumatized person can become withdrawn, avoidant or even afraid to leave the house at times. Trauma can make someone become timid and can consume their motivation or ability to make decisions and move forward in life.

We are naturally attracted to repeating our trauma, especially when it comes to relationships. The butterflies that we feel when we first meet someone are not necessarily a feeling of first love — it is often an indicator that the body is reacting in fight or flight, telling us that the individual is not the right match. When this occurs, the feeling you have is reflecting the same energetic signature of your mother or father. It feels like love, even if it is dysfunctional or conditional, because it is all that you know. When this happens, you are bonding with your trauma and not with the person in front of you. You are attempting to bond with one or both of your parents — looking for love in all the wrong people.

FORGIVE AND FORGET

According to Harjiwan, a teacher from the Kundalini Yoga heritage, we need a forgive-and-forget strategy to heal our trauma. Some people can go through a lot of pain in their lives and easily integrate it in order to move on. Most people cannot, and the trauma inverts on them, creating a specific lens to experience the world and the storyline of their life. These individuals become addicted to the feelings that were created by the traumatic experience and the energy surrounding it. They repeat the past over and over — constantly recycling the same trash. This is because they are literally putting out a vibratory signal to recreate the past in the present.

I know this because I have experienced it — and I have healed. I have also seen many of my clients recognize how their past trauma sneaks into the present — and they choose to take a different road. You have to forgive, forget, and move on to do this. Forgiving gives you a chance at living your best life. Forgetting is for your own salvation. You must move forward from the trauma and not focus on it, because once you focus on something, you create more thoughts about it, which is not beneficial. You are an alchemist and I want to teach you how to increase your frequency so that you can live your best life.

When I left my husband, I began to go through a profound experience of healing the pain around my heart. The wounded feminine is a common template on our planet, but the Divine Feminine is a template that is being newly constructed and birthed into form. The contractions hurt. We do not really know what a woman in her full power or worth looks like and each of us has the opportunity to design what that means in our lives now. Healing is not selfish. It is done for your children so you can be a better mother and for generations going backward and forward.

I was designing an entirely new template of what it meant to be a self-sovereign woman — something no one in my family had ever done — which felt like a daunting and impossible task. Before I could really understand this, I had to release the heavy load that was holding me back from living my full destiny. A part of this healing process was finding out more about myself through dating. As I began to date a series of different categories of men, I was in shock at all the barriers and gaps I was experiencing between myself and finding love. I saw different aspects of my father in each of these categories and as my trauma healed, I saw a significant improvement in the type of men I attracted.

An important part of gaining self-worth and self-love while dating is learning to say no, moving on, and trusting that the Universe will always bring you something better. You have to do the internal work to change your life and frequency, which takes consistent devotion. This is true for your career and many other aspects of creating your best life. If you are currently in a relationship or career that you are unhappy with, you do not have to leave to do the internal work. In fact, if you do leave you will recreate it until the pattern is changed within. I used the technology of Kundalini Yoga and Meditation as taught by Yogi Bhajan in combination with honoring the phases of the alchemical process to change my frequency. I had to grow in all areas of my life — money, career, as a mother, a home owner, traveler, healer, and international author — before I could really understand what love was.

As young children, we are not taught how to nourish our self-worth. If anything, we are put down for our weight, clothes, hair, personality, and even intelligence. There is a lot to deprogram. Nor do many of us have a template for what a healthy relationship looks like. Women are generally not taught about red flags in relationships — who we should walk away from or how to spot men that are not healthy for us (even if we are married to them). I had to learn this through trial and error and I hope to save you some of the pain by laying it out in this book. Remember, if you are experiencing something in another and it is dramatically affecting your emotional body, the same characteristics live within you.

We are all involved in healing the Divine Masculine on this Earth by healing ourselves. In order to change yourself, increase your quality of life, and experience a better-quality relationship, you have to sift through your psyche. This is easier to do when you have the reflection of others in your life to show you what you need to work through.

CHAPTER FOUR: SEPARATION

GETTING TO KNOW YOURSELF

Once mental rigidity has been released through Dissolution, the alchemist must learn to separate out the parts of his or her personality that are no longer appropriate for continued growth. By this point, the individual has recognized that past trauma is sneaking into the present, but they have to make the conscious decision not to continue to allow toxic behavior in themselves or around them through others. This is a stage of separating out what you want to create in your life from what you do not. You have to choose to have a better experience and what kind of experience you want to create. It is really hard to let go of destructive habits that were created as a result of the past. It is especially hard to see how far away from real love we are.

When someone goes through traumatic events, they are often paralyzed by these experiences mentally, emotionally, and spiritually. You can see the trauma in the distortions of the face when it is not symmetrical and you can hear the sound of trauma in a voice when the pitch changes. Though a person looks a certain age, it does not mean that he or she is actually acting their age. Individuals typically get stunted at the age their trauma occurred and never really grow up. Couples often partner to work out their pain and when they disagree, they regress to the ages where they were both traumatized or developmentally stunted at. Though a couple may be in their forties from an outside perspective, they may actually be functioning at the level of teenagers in many aspects of their lives. They, in turn, parent their children from this age, creating another generation just like them. Children can't consciously raise children.

The stage of Separation is the point in time where the individual must choose to begin to grow up. To do this, it is necessary to separate out the childish, toxic, neurotic, and phobic parts of the personality in order to grow into a higher functioning human being. The alchemist will start to consciously confront parts of themselves that were previously unknown and own up to the mistakes they have made throughout life. The alchemist knows that he or she cannot control the external world and recognizes that the only thing he or she has control of is the internal environment. He or she must essentially heal and raise the wounded children within by learning how to parent him or herself.

As an alchemist, it is necessary to determine the kind of experience you want to create on Earth and decide if you want to live from a place of chaos or peace. During this phase, you will have a clearer understanding of the weaknesses within your personality and be able to decide what kind of baggage you are willing to hold onto for yourself and others. This is the point in time where boundaries become important and you will learn to say no to people and environments that are unsafe or toxic. You will also stop trying to conquer the external world because you are beginning to notice the negative masculine parts of your personality. Domineering, forceful, and abusive tendencies will begin to become apparent both within yourself and through the reflection provided by your relationships. It is necessary to separate out the ungenuine, shameful or unworthy material from your life to become a whole human being.

NOTICING THE RED FLAGS

When red flags arise in relationships, they are often ignored because these types of behaviors were normalized in your childhood and remain unhealed within. Red flags in relationships are warning signs that the relationship does not hold healthy dynamics or boundaries. These signs can be subtle or overt and range from forms of abuse, to manipulation, to games or drama. If you were programmed with these unhealthy relationship dynamics as a child, or associated this behavior as normal from your caretakers, these red flags become easily excusable as an adult. Individuals will often stay with a partner and play out these wounds over and over again until they heal the underlying childhood program.

As an alchemist, you must become good at identifying your original wounds and how they play out in your relationships. Do not be overwhelmed at how many wounds you have or how long they take to heal. Know that if Spirit is guiding, you will likely begin to meet exactly who you are supposed to meet to heal at a faster rate than the average person. Relationships are an excellent way to wake up your consciousness because they are a direct mirror to the parts of yourself that you need to work on. The more you recognize your own self-sabotage, or the way you create personal chaos, the faster you can move through any given issue within a relationship dynamic.

When we form a relationship, there are many dynamics at work: expectations, childhood conditioning — and especially feelings. The initial attraction is what often draws you and another together, and bonding depends on the way that you were raised. Your level of attachment may look very different from that of someone who was raised with an alternative program around love. If you experience butterflies, love at first sight or move too quickly when you meet someone, you may be recognizing your trauma in another.

Be wary as you are likely not bonding to the individual but to the chaotic pattern that lies within that person. You feel at home: you have met your mother or father in a new body. Until you have healed the parts of yourself that keep walking into the fire, you will keep reexperiencing your childhood through these relationships. This initial attraction will often pull you into a fantasy projection of what a relationship is or a living nightmare.

AVOIDING POTENTIALLY DANGEROUS RELATIONSHIPS

Sandra Brown wrote *How to Spot a Dangerous Man Before You Get Involved* to help women identify potentially dangerous relationships. She has worked with thousands of women — many who were highly educated and successful — teaching them how to not compromise their well-being or personal safety for another. Her work helps women identify red flags in behavior so that they can quickly recognize the negative pattern and choose to walk away with their dignity and sanity. Her book describes characteristics of personalities that are considered dangerous and extremely volatile. She created a comprehensive list of qualities to avoid when choosing to be in relationship with a man. These include:

- The Man who Clings
- The Parental Seeker
- The Emotionally Unavailable Man

- The Man with the Hidden Life

- A Mentally Ill Man

- The Addict

- An Abusive or Violent Man

- The Emotional Predator

I am purposely choosing not to go into detail with each of these characteristics because this is Sandra Brown's material (which I encourage you to read) and because this book is not a manifesto against the male. *Alchemy of Becoming* is a book to help you heal the wounded parts of yourself that attracted this type of energy into your life through your own thoughts. The biggest takeaway that I read is that you cannot heal these red flags in the male. If you are used to being the healer, or you were the parent to your mother or father, entering into these types of relationships is very tempting because of the familiarity. I want you to forgive, forget, and move on — and this requires consistent letting go. Choosing to be in a relationship with someone on Brown's list will loop you into trauma and drama, and as an alchemist you have a much bigger purpose than just trying to heal one person. Brown explains that these red flags are sociopathic, and neurologically ingrained. You cannot change these types of men and I have to tell you I agree with her

100 percent. You can only change yourself by not allowing them in your life.

Maya Angelou said, "When someone shows you who they are, believe them the first time." This cannot be more accurate when identifying who to spend your time with. If someone shows you that they lie, are undependable, have a pervasive lifestyle, are untrustworthy, cruel or abusive, do not think that they will suddenly change for you. You have to be with the man in front of you, not the man you hope he will become. The more you learn to say no to sociopathic men, the more your self-esteem will grow and you will begin to attract higher caliber males that honor and respect you. Of course, there are always dynamics in the relationship that need to be worked out. Know that the more that you move into your Divine Feminine, the more you will begin to initiate the men around you to move into their Divine Masculine. By growing into your self-worth, you will inevitably ask the men in your life to upgrade with you. By acknowledging your inner Beloved, you will move into sacred union.

SEPARATING FROM THE PAIN

I want to be very clear that these characteristics are just samples of the human experience. Do not get interlocked with these personalities or if you do, don't stay with them. These human experiences exist, but I want you to get to a place where, if you encounter anyone like this and feel triggered, you do not react or get hooked into playing out the pattern. You just walk away. These characteristics are in both women and men. Women create, birth, and raise men. Every quality within a man first comes from the woman. If you experience any of those qualities in Brown's list in a relationship, look at the aspect of the mother who birthed the man and the father who may have helped raise him. Question the history and personality of the mother and look into her wounds, for they programmed him in the womb. Then take a deeper look into your past, to see where your patterns are similar, in order to understand why you came together.

I am not providing you this list of qualities to make you scared. I do not want you to immediately leave your marriage, become angry or avoid dating. I am also not stating that all men are dangerous. But I do want you to begin to recognize who is in front of you and have an honest and accurate interpretation of your reality. Many people spend a lifetime living in ignorance and completely avoid the fact that they are not happy. Instead of relating to the person at hand, they relate to some version of what they hope this person could become, thus creating a story that is an illusion. This is because the individual does not feel whole or complete without a partner and is attempting to fill internal lack through a relationship.

Individuals commonly project from the positive mind, focusing on the best qualities of another, and that may not be accurate. It is also common to swing the other way and project negativity by focusing on all the terrible parts of a person. Reactions vary depending on the mind, emotions, and the programming from the past. What your mind focuses on is what you will create. My hope is that you will begin to see from the neutral mind — you see the person for who they are in front of you in the moment. When you do this, you are not living from your past or designing your reality based on what you hope the future will be.

I had a client who was with a man who exemplified several of the types of men in Brown's list. He lived a secret underground life involving sexual deviance (humiliation and occasionally pain) and wearing women's clothing. This secret life took over his thoughts and desire. He held a great amount of shame around his sexuality and alternative lifestyle which was likely passed down through the womb (a concept I discuss in depth in *Mystical Motherhood* and *Fertile*). His mother was sexually abused as a child by her brother — this was her original wound. When this happened, her mother, likely knowing that the wound occurred, never apologized or discussed the trauma. She sent her daughter away to boarding school, essentially banishing her from the family. The brother was allowed to take over the family business, marry, start a family and was never confronted for his behavior.

When my client left this man as a result of his sexual deviancy, she was close to his mother, who was ignorant of her son's secret lifestyle. My client shared what she could to the mother without breaking confidentiality, and she repeated the exact same behavior to my client that her mother had done to her. She refused to fully acknowledge what happened between my client and her son. She emotionally banished my client from her life and encouraged her son to move on in relationship and business. She did this completely unconsciously, even though what her mother had done to her was one of the deepest pains of her life. This story shows that the original wound will always conspire to repeat itself until confronted and healed. Neither the son nor his mother was aware of the other's original wounds, which held them back from fully experiencing their hearts. This is what we refer to as family on this planet. We find solace and familiarity in the places where our wounds link together.

Another client's husband was unable to hold a job for long because he would self-sabotage and quit whenever he began to create stability in his life. He was also always in debt because he never received the template from his father, who was in and out of jail for stealing, on how to be responsible. As a grown man, he was used to women taking care of him financially because his mother always did. He saw his father lying and as an adult could not articulate truth, so he created a projected reality of a false persona. Clearly, this type of man didn't know better because he didn't have the parental figures to teach him. If you feel any familiarity with any of these types of personalities, you shouldn't teach them either.

It is not your responsibility to mother a man. You should only mother your own children and you can do this much better by knowing how to mother yourself. If you do try to mother or heal a male, he will likely despise you for it and project his own unhealed wounds back on to you. I have had many clients like the two just described with various stories and family templates that needed healing. It wasn't until they began to work with me that they were able to see that their current patterns could be tracked back in time to their childhood and even as far back as their grandmothers. Wounds are passed down, generation after generation, without conscious awareness that the conditioning even exists. This distance from the truth is called ignorance. It is my life's work through the Mystical Motherhood platform and book series to help heal these wounds within every woman who is ready to come to the realization that they have the power to birth a new reality on Earth.

HOW TO BEGIN HEALING

Separation is the alchemical stage where we look at the rejected parts of the personality. We take a deeper dive into the pain or hidden parts of ourselves that we didn't think existed and then decide that we are ready to release the patterns. Now is the time to separate out what you want in your life and what you do not. It is the time to begin to create the life you desire by breaking old habits and cutting away things that no longer serve you.

If your original wounds are around substance abuse, you may need to cut out people who partake in these activities or stop yourself. If you have wounds around overworking, it is time to observe this pattern and change it. Separation is when we begin the process of letting go of what we are most attached to. Anger, resentment, grief, loss, and frustration may arise as you learn to make boundaries and say no to people, places, and activities that are not in your best interest. If you notice these feelings, they are indications that you are really just mad at yourself for allowing the behavior to prevail in your life for so long. Do not use this period of time to play victim: you must now rise up as a spiritual warrior.

Months after leaving my husband and many dates later, I realized that I was attracting men like my dad in my life. Though I should not have been dating, my wound needed to be fed. My father was haunting me and I wasn't even aware of his ghost until I sat across from him in New York restaurants. I heard his voice through their mental disability and received his neglect when they didn't text or call me back regularly. I felt the pain of his rejection and abandonment when the men I was dating could not show me the love I deserved. I met him in the man that lied about his life, the one that cheated on his wife, the man who only wanted to text me and would not take me out, and the one who just wanted sex. I saw him through the man that talked over me and manipulated my words. My experience was dreamlike and my nightmare was dictated by the past. I was so conditioned that I had no real freedom. As I awakened from this dream, I had to separate out my thoughts that were obsessed with the negativity in men.

The little girl within me wanted love from Dad so badly that she was willing to stay with men similar to him with the hopes that one day they would change. The little girl was attempting to heal her core wound by attracting men that had not emotionally matured. My little girl wanted to stay in Neverland with Peter Pan and help him grow up. However, it was time to leave this fantasy and grow into the educated and beautiful woman I saw in the mirror. I knew I could do better. I began to utilize Sandra Brown's work to weed out the men that I could not date. It was very hard to separate from such a deeply ingrained pattern, but over time I learned to say no and walk away when any red flags arose. Because if there was one red flag, it wasn't long until more would come. As I did this, I began to trust myself more.

I also did specific meditations from the Kundalini Yoga heritage as taught by Yogi Bhajan. (*Mystical Motherhood* talks about the benefit of this practice in general and provides many other resources. You can go to the Mystical Motherhood website to learn how to do these so that you can heal too.) The Separation phase of the awakening process showed me exactly what I could not allow in my life. My true awakening began as I saw that the only reasons these men were in my vicinity were because I was allowing it and my unhealed subconscious patterns were attracting it. If I accepted emotional unavailability, neglect, and mental disability, that energy had to reside somewhere within me. The Kundalini Meditations I completed helped to eliminate these patterns within me and, as I began to heal, the little girls that needed love began to grow up. I then moved into the Conjunction phase of the alchemical transformation.

CHAPTER FIVE: CONJUNCTION

COMING TOGETHER

Conjunction is the stage of awakening where much of the pain of the heart has subsided. Life flows with more ease and there is less intensity as you experience neutrality within extreme polarities. Emotions were released through Dissolution, and the mental thoughts that once took over your life begin to have less control. Though thoughts have not completely dissipated, there is more joy in what you create in your life in this phase. This is a time when the alchemist begins to touch into living from the essence of the heart energy in a balanced way.

Before Conjunction, much of the alchemist's time is spent experiencing consciousness that moves back and forth between the mind and the heart, creating depression mixed with moments of elation. The pain that one experiences as the heart begins to open is because the person must let go of all of the egoic structures that keep him or her earthbound or in the lower three chakras. He or she must release the human story that is created in the mind. These stories contain similar content for most people — they include attachments to people, sexual perversions, issues around material wealth or scarcity, power dynamics, or trauma. The story I tell within this book is my original wound. Yours may be very different or quite similar. Conjunction is the point in time you begin to really let go of your story so that you can work with the higher aspects of yourself and the Divine.

The pain of holding your attachment to the human story feels like a crucifixion. The biggest difference between you and Christ is that you put yourself on the cross and you are the only one who can take yourself off. When you come off, you will look back at the cross and see what it signifies: the ignorance, insensitivity, and illusions we all bind ourselves to within our own pain. As the alchemist becomes more balanced, these attachments slowly begin to become less important. Though they have not completely subsided at this stage of development, the desire of the heart to feel more peace and tranquility becomes predominant.

Because you no longer have a cross to carry around, you can more easily see what needs to be changed in your life to create truth. Up until this time, you really do not know who you are, because you are filled with so many ideas of who you think you should be, and they are based on the conditioning from your past. During Conjunction, your life comes together as the male and female aspects within combine in a healthy manner. This may be reflected in your living situation, career, or even friendships. This is the stage where the alchemist grows up and begins to feel more self-worth and regard. Where you once may have accepted negativity or neglect, this is a period of time where you move into the heart, which wants to create love and belonging.

STEPS TO BECOMING WHOLE

I was doing a lot of work on myself to raise my self-esteem by beginning to not date men that fit the categories discussed in the previous section. I was meditating daily, working with healers consistently, and going to every White Tantria Yoga event I could attend, to heal the pattern within. White Tantra Yoga is a meditation event that lasts all day and creates a great deal of healing in a short period of time. Many people say that it is the most powerful technology for spiritual acceleration available on the planet.

Other parts of my life were taking off too. I published *Fertile*, was growing in my career as a Reproductive Nurse Practitioner, and my children were flourishing. (I want to note here that my children did not meet the men I was dating, except for one which was longer term. I highly recommend not introducing children to anyone until you know they will be a part of your life and healthy for your children's.) I was hired at a fertility clinic called Genesis in Brooklyn. Remember the significance of the story of Adam and Eve from the section of Genesis in the Bible? The word Genesis also breaks down to "Genes of Isis", which was an important concept discussed in *Fertile*. The Goddess Isis has always been an archetypal guide for me on my journey.

I had sent the clinic Genesis my resume even though they did not have a position open and had never hired a Nurse Practitioner in the past. I did not even consider the significance of the name until months after starting. After I was hired, I began to train with one of the best doctors in the fertility field named Dr. Grazi. On my first day, I walked into his exam room and saw a large painting of the Goddess Isis on the wall, which did not fit into the rest of the décor of the two-story center. I said, "Dr. Grazi, do you know that the Goddess Isis is one of the original birthers? Do you know who she is and why you have this painting on your wall?" He said, "I have no idea." God works in mysterious ways. I just keep following that internal guidance system that gives me winks when I am headed in the right direction.

Not being in a dedicated relationship allowed my career to flourish. I was growing in all parts of my life, yet I was still occasionally attracting men with aspects of my father and the past. Though I had learned to let go of them and say no, next I had to heal the pattern that actually attracted them. I

CHAPTER FIVE: CONJUNCTION

needed to fully protect myself and leave my story behind. One day, as I was walking and wasn't paying attention, I hit a wall, literally, and collapsed to the floor while crying out loud, "Please God, just heal me. Get this out of me. I am ready to really change now."

A short time thereafter, I was texting with a friend and I asked if she had ever practiced yoga with a teacher named Guru Dharam or knew when his next course would be. This name suddenly appeared in my mind — I had recently been flipping through a photo book called *Yoga* and had seen his picture. My friend told me that she believed he was teaching a class on relationships in New York that weekend, which I found hard to believe because he is a teacher that is known worldwide and usually travels. I looked online and found that he and his wife, Siri Sat, were in fact teaching a course on relationships that weekend and it started in exactly one hour. I did not have work that day, my children were with their father, and I had no set plans that weekend. I called to see if they had space and heard, "Yes, we even printed one extra course book."

When the alchemist calls out, the Universe will listen, but not everyone responds when the call for action appears. It takes the same amount of energy to sit in your pain as to heal it. I chose the latter, even though I could have equally made excuses as to why I couldn't make it to an intensive course that started in one hour. In the experience, I learned some specific meditations including the Mera Man Lochai for healing the wounds of the heart and the So Purkh prayer to heal the Divine

Masculine. (These meditations are described in detail in a course available on the Mystical Motherhood website.) I committed to doing these meditations for three months or longer, daily.

Within a week of starting the course, I began to converse with a man who was kind, conscious, communicable, respectful, peaceful, responsible, and loving. I had never met a man that held all of these qualities within one body. After leaving a date with him, I went home and began to dance in joy. I didn't know if this would be the man I would end up with, but I knew that I had finally broken the pattern within myself of attracting my father. From that point forward, as I came into balance internally, I began to casually date higher caliber men who were more interested in spirituality and growth.

As I was healing, I created a symbol of the sacred relationship I desired, which was two birds and a rose garden. Birds randomly came to mind at the time I chose my symbol, but I can see clearly now that the bird was also the symbol of my father. (You'll remember the significance of his name and the blackbird?) The blackbird coincidentally is also a symbol in the alchemical transformation. Alchemists know that the Universe is always speaking, especially through symbols, music, numbers, and conversations.

When I went on a date with the man I just mentioned, my sister, not knowing my symbol, sent me a picture of two birds nesting in a rose garden. I read later that two birds nesting is also the symbol of the phase of Conjunction in alchemy. I was in constant dialogue with the Universe throughout my process of healing and I learned to listen and trust, even when it hurt. Signs and symbols tell you both when you are on track and when to walk away. Whenever I was in the wrong relationship, I would see a dead bird on my path and if I tried to ignore it in hopes the Universe was wrong, I would see another.

Though I was thankful to finally break the spell of dating unconscious men, I was still yearning for love. I was looking for love from a partner, hoping that this individual could fulfill me. We can only attract our vibrational match though. If you feel any lack inside, or that something is missing, you will attract individuals who are also experiencing scarcity. During the Conjunction phase though, I did enjoy experiencing my growing internal balance reflected back to me through various men I casually dated. I was not in a state of complete satisfaction yet, because none of the individuals I was dating could provide me the union I so desired. I still had more growing up to do, parts of myself to let go of, and polarities within that had to come into balance at this stage of awakening.

GROWING UP

In order to move into the Conjunction stage of awakening, an individual must have become whole. As I mentioned before, trauma or disruptions from our past can stunt our behavior and personality.

Individuals typically function at, or regress to, the age that their perceived trauma occurred and live their life looping the same issues, unable to accelerate forward.

Individuals often project their thoughts, lack, and issues onto their partners. Each person hopes that the other will change so they can individually be happy. When this is the state of affairs, there is growing up to do on a personal level. Both the male and the female need to heal at the ages where the original wounds occurred. The little girl within you needs to be satiated or she will regress to a needy, anxious, emotional, and neurotic mess when triggered. Because she is a living and functioning subconscious pattern that affects your daily life, she will demand to be fed first. If you had a lot of bad memories or consistent pain throughout childhood, you have to heal all of the little girls at various ages in order to grow up.

Healing these children can take a lifetime; for many alchemists, who go through the awakening process at a hyperspeed, it can take a few months to years. As you begin the journey of healing, you will go through a personal resurrection. By touching into the innocence of the little children within you, and bringing back their original joy, you will begin to feel the Kingdom of Heaven on Earth. The hard part about this is that you must go through a spiritual death to get back to your original nature and purity. This is the point in time that you realize you were never really nailed to the cross, but could get off at any moment. As I previously mentioned, during Conjunction you will move from your heart to your head and back again until you settle into your heart.

EXPERIENCING POLARITIES

Another important stage of Conjunction is coming into balance with the polarities that are both inside and outside of us. The heart is a neutral energy center, and settling into this place requires internal balance and nonreaction to the polarities that exist on this planet. I have spoken about polarities before and will reference a few examples again here, such as male and female, light and dark, and attachment and avoidance. The alchemical process helps to reduce overall reactions to any life stressors. When you begin to navigate the world around you from your heart, rather than your mind, there is nothing left to fight. The outside world is highly affected by polarities, but a real alchemist is not affected by external experiences because everything is created internally — specifically the experience of peace, tranquility, and love. Coming into this centered, neutral, and contained space within is an essential step as you move towards nonreaction and into Conjunction.

According to Yogi Bhajan, there are three types of love:

Attachment: *The drive to be close to someone else.*

Passion: *The drive for sexuality or the urge to mate.*

Intimacy: *The drive for personal exchanges, mutual disclosure, and recognition.*

These attributes of a relationship are not always in equal proportion and sometimes only one component is active within the partnership. Once the initial attraction arises, you will begin to create a reaction within the relationship dynamic at some point, based on your subconscious patterns. This is the point at which one or both partners may regress to a younger age as previously discussed. If the couple is not in a calm and neutral place internally, they will approach the relationship actively or passively and experience the polarity of their reaction. Each of the types of love listed above has an opposite reaction.

If you were never modeled proper attachment growing up, as it increases within a relationship, you may increasingly feel the fear of abandonment. Or, on the other end of that spectrum, you may push love away and become unavailable. If you associate love with abandonment, you will naturally pick a partner that will help recreate that wound — or you will recreate the wound within yourself. (Remember we create our reality, and our heart-opening process is ultimately done by us for our soul's growth.) If sexuality is very prominent in your relationship, you may eventually feel the polarity of this highly expressed emotion, which would be boredom or disinterest.

Secure attachment is one of the most important components within an individual and within a relationship. Your level of adult attachment is dependent on the type of relationship you had with your parents. According to Amir Levine and Rachel Heller, authors of *Attached*, there are three types of attachment: secure, anxious, and avoidant. Secure individuals are very comfortable with becoming intimate. Anxious individuals crave intimacy to the point of feeling abandonment, worry, and obsession. Avoidant individuals do not like getting close to others, and create scenarios to minimize intimacy. Anxious and avoidant people tend to come together in relationship and are attached to each other's traumas, each one feeding the other's pain.

Discussing security in relationships is beyond the scope of this book, but it is one of the most important parts of healing and finding love. I highly encourage you to read *Attached* as a healing tool in your journey to opening your heart. I can tell you from personal experience that if you have an anxious attachment style, you cannot be happy with an avoidant personality, even though you will be powerfully drawn to this person. You only feel attracted to them because it plays out your childhood dynamics. Despite the fact that an avoidant "avoids" intimacy, they also prefer to be with a person who has an anxious attachment style. Underneath it all, they do want love, but lack the emotional or mental ability to handle it. Neither type of attachment style was provided security, emotional safety, or unconditional love as a child. Both are very capable of healing to become secure.

There are more avoidants available to date because they do not like to bond, but you can learn to walk away and find security in a relationship. If you have an anxious attachment style and are currently with an avoidant, you may not even be aware of the dynamic because you are too busy trying to receive love, stuck as you are in the story of playing out your original wound. Again, this is an example of trying to receive the love you did not get as a child. The only way to heal is to become emotionally secure and happy within yourself. Putting yourself first creates sovereignty and requires letting go of society's programming that this is selfish.

Alchemists are on this planet to serve humanity, and the ability to do this comes from a never-ending internal energy that is connected to Source. If you are constantly giving your love out to others who do not respect, honor, and cherish you, you are not only wasting precious time and energy, but you are potentially ruining your mission to help the people who really want it. You do not owe anyone an explanation for not allowing them to access your flow of energy. If you desire to be around someone that does not fully appreciate you or treats you badly, you are playing out an unhealed wound. You must learn to say no, walk away, or create boundaries, even if this involves family members. When you start to create this level of self-love, the Universe will come in to test you to ensure that your thoughts are pure and your heart is truly healed. This is the next stage of the alchemical process that the alchemist must go through to find The One.

CHAPTER SIX: FERMENTATION AND PUTREFACTION

THE POWER OF IMAGINATION

Once an alchemist is balanced on the earthly plane, he or she will begin to move up and down the vertical ladder of time and dimensions to create a connection in various planes of existence. Alchemists bring higher ideas down to be solidified and actualized on Earth. During this phase of alchemy, one learns the power and the fire of the imagination. This is a period where you may experience shamanic worlds, the paranormal, or psychic phenomena.

Dennis Hauck refers to these shamanic visions as the "peacock's tail," which is represented by the colors of the rainbow. I believe that the rainbow is symbolic during this phase of awakening, because all of the colors within the mind paint your outside world. Hauck says, "Fermentation is accomplished through what alchemists called the True Imagination — a state of consciousness in which mental images or visions seem more representative of reality than anything that we can see with our eyes. It is as if our consciousness has left the bounds of matter and exists outside our bodies, and everything we experience in this state is more real and more truthful than the everyday world."[1] This phase pushes the initiate to know that there are no earthly limitations to creating except except those imposed by the ego.

This is the phase where you will truly learn that your thoughts create action in the world with great precision. If your thoughts are filled with ego, personal desire, past conditions or subconscious programming, they are not in alignment with Source, and as a result will reflect this impurity. This is the stage where the alchemist must begin to let go of the egoic-driven personality for good, and start the process of fully surrendering to God to create, from the heart center, the purest manifestations in the earthly realm. Before this stage of development, you will feel a darkness and heaviness, but as you are lifted into the higher realms through the power of your imagination, you literally become light. From this, great works of art can be created or manifested for the benefit of humanity.

THE ILLUSIONS OF THE EGO

The purpose of Fermentation and Putrefaction is to create purity within so that you can co-create with the One Mind, which is Source — and not from your personal egoic mind. The ego is selfish and likes personal gratification. It is the part of you that pushes, grasps, and desires. This unsettled aspect is constantly moving forward in a dominant and demanding way. The ego says, "I want it now, I want it to be my way and I will fight to get it." Throughout my life I have always had a difficult time telling the difference between my ego and the feminine part of me that is guided by Source to continually create and expand. It took the period of Fermentation and Putrefaction for me to understand the difference in desires.

The ego is future driven, always focusing on creating a goal that is not based in reality — and reality is what is happening in the present moment. It is the part of you that becomes obsessed with arriving at the desired action and loses the joy of the creation. If you are in balance in your Divine Feminine, an ease and an ecstatic motion come through your creations. This flow guides you through miracles and surprises that are not based in the logical mind. There may be a few natural obstacles that present themselves when you are creating something with this type of energy, but they won't be as great as when you are manifesting from the level of the ego or mind.

If the future becomes more important than what is happening right now, you have a problem. If everything that you are doing is focused on creating something that is not here and now, you are in your ego. This desire will feel like something in the future is going to make you feel more complete, finally happy, or whole. The energy of this is grasping, stressful, fearful, active, manipulative, and frustrating. Nothing will flow with ease, and you will find many obstacles in your way. This type of journey is intense and not very pleasant because you are so focused on getting what you want. You are basically postponing enjoying your life, because you think that something else is going to be better.

MANIFESTING FROM THE MIND

I wanted a relationship so desperately with the masculine that I created a timeline as to when it would arrive: I convinced myself, with the help of all my "psychic" friends, that he would meet me in March, 2020. Up until that very special month, I was looking for him everywhere. I spent months in desperate preparation just in case he showed up early. I looked for him at museums, in restaurants, on streets, and on dating websites. I wanted to be held, cherished, and loved. March arrived, and coincidentally this was the same month the entire world around me shut down at an extreme level. March 2020 was the month that the coronavirus hit the United States. Nothing like this had ever occurred on our planet in written history. I just so happened to be living in one of the most populated parts of the world that was hit the hardest.

The virus moved across the ocean and swept through New York City hospitals like a wave of destruction during the same time that I had convinced myself my life partner would arrive. It all happened very fast: everything was completely shut down within a few days and the city that never sleeps was forced to shelter in place. People were asked to not leave their homes, and businesses were shut down completely, to the point that there were no cars on the busiest roads and no one in the New York subway stations.

Despite the fact that the world was falling down around me, I was sure I would meet my beloved partner — so sure that I willed it into action. I knew he would arrive in March because I saw it in my imagination. He was tall, dark, and handsome — of course. In my vision, he wore a black beanie because it was still relatively cold outside. I saw us meeting in the park and he showed me the number three which I thought meant the third month of the year. I was living for this vision, and various others that I will soon discuss, for many months. Almost everyone in New York was forced to stay at home, but one day when there was sunlight out, a friend asked me to meet her at the park. This was the end of March and one of the very last days that I could possibly meet my partner.

Sure enough, there he was, walking by and looking just like I had seen him in my vision. I was sitting down and listening to music. We saw each other and, because of the music, began our conversation. We learned that we had children the same age and the same birthday! Who could have imagined such a coincidence? Well, I did. I imagined it into reality despite the fact that we were asked to wear masks, maintain a distance of six feet apart and to remain cordial and not in extreme panic during an international pandemic. I made it happen! Over the next few days to weeks, we began to get to know each other and I told him straight away what I knew for sure — that he was The One I had been waiting for. I explained that my prayer was to meet my beloved partner who would help take me to my highest destiny. It was only fair to be honest.

When he told me that he was not this man that I had so hoped to meet in the park, I was in shock. I explained that I saw him coming for months and it must be him, but he wasn't sure how he could manage to take me to my highest destiny as he had a lot to work on within himself. Once I dropped the projection of what my ego wanted this man to be, I could clearly see the man in front of me. He was a man about fifteen years older than me who was mentally disturbed by the mistakes of his past, who needed someone to heal him. As I got to know him better, I saw that he didn't know how to take care of himself very well and was emotionally avoidant and financially suffering. He told me that he had asked God to send him someone to save him and then I arrived. The man that sat in front of me was my father.

CHAPTER SIX: FERMENTATION AND PUTREFACTION

There he was again, my dad, back from the dead asking me to heal him. The level of depression that hit me after I realized I had manifested another aspect of my father is indescribable. All I ever desired was love from a partner, yet these partners could not provide that love. Though this man was conscious, kind, and loving, he still held a similar energetic frequency to parts of my past. I desired so deeply to be partnered and cherished by a man that I willed it into reality — only to find that it was not what I was looking for. The hole within began to widen and I fell into a deep depression. The pressure that the coronavirus put on the world at that time helped to bring up the last remnants of my subconscious desires. I entered into the Putrefaction phase of alchemical transformation where I began to objectively witness the ways in which I was causing my own despair and depression.

Hauck said, "During psychological death or putrefaction, the 'child' of the Conjunction, which is the strongest presence you can create within your earthbound personality, is exposed to the decadent humidity of your deepest and most clinging psychic components, the psychological manure in which most of us wallow."[2] I could finally see just how clearly this original wound was dictating my life and driving my need to find love outside myself. The difference between this stage and the previous stages of alchemy is that I was able to see my patterns without completely being consumed by them, as is the case during Dissolution. I also didn't project it back on this man — a lesson I learned in Calcination.

The alchemical stage of Fermentation breaks down belief systems completely. It collapses your past. A catalyst may naturally arrive in your life in some form to give you an entirely new outlook on a situation. This is the stage that we finally and truly understand why we act a certain way, and we begin the process of surrender. During Fermentation I began to stop identifying with the pain, and my sense of Self shifted. I witnessed my story from an outside view and with an objective presence, and then I began the process of letting it go. I stopped identifying with my mental thoughts and experienced what Hauck described as the peacock's tail: I had visions which showed me the exact layout of this book. I did not even know that I had been going through an alchemical transformation until this point, because I could not objectively fully separate from the pain that my story caused.

That day, visions manifested in my head which helped me to see how my personal transformation could create a piece of art in the form of a book. The pain of my past began to physically birth through me as I wrote *Alchemy of Becoming*. I turned truth into power and fear into love. The Putrefaction stage turned the deepest darkness into the greatest light. As the light poured through within minutes to hours, I saw the entire layout and content of this book. How this happened is hard to describe, but it was as if a rainbow of color began to create an art piece. Within a few months, this book was birthed — out of nothing. Words flowed through me as I objectively witnessed my story so that others could objectively witness theirs.

In order to produce something with love, I had to witness where my flow of energy was going. I had spent most of my life worrying or thinking about men. All of my love and attention was directed towards pleasing another with the hopes that that would make me happy. This is all I knew to focus on, and where thoughts flow, actions follow. I needed to learn how to stop giving my love away so easily because, when I did, there was nothing left for me or my creative pursuits. I recognized how depleted I was and that I needed time to heal. I began to see how much energy I was losing by focusing my mind on a future relationship. Because I had shifted that love back inside of me, this book flowed through me with ease. My next challenge was: I had to work through the ways in which I sabotaged my own success.

STOPPING SELF-SABOTAGE

When your mind stops creating problems, life becomes very peaceful. Alchemists know that all problems are self-created. Of course, there are times when issues arise and problems must be solved for yourself or another, but humans do not need to be constantly anxious or emotional. If you take some time to reflect back on your life, you may see just how many of your problems were self-created, even though you blamed someone or something outside of yourself. If this is the case, you can usually follow your negative mind stream back in time to clearly see the types of problems you prefer to create.

It is necessary to differentiate between whether you really have a problem at hand or whether you are contributing to the problem. Most of the time it is the latter. When I work with clients, I go back in their timeline and find the original belief system and wound that contribute to their mental thoughts and anxiety. For example, if you have a control issue around food, food may be all that you think about. Your mind may even trick you into believing that you are doing yourself a favor by focusing on your health. You may become obsessed with cooking vegan, gluten-free or eating vegetables. You believe you are eating clean and you associate this with health, but if the thoughts turn to obsession, it is not healthy. What you may not be able to see is that these thoughts around food are taking up a significant amount of time and energy. When your mind is consumed by something, it is a result of a conditioning from your childhood or your mother's womb. The key is to let go of the conditioning you have around your attachment to food, and notice how your mind creates a story to keep the obsession going. Food is just one example of many mental intrigues.

Another important quality of an alchemist is to notice where you are losing your energy. When things start to become calm and peaceful in your life, what are the ways that you begin to create chaos? If you are used to a certain level of drama, trauma or anxiety, and when life becomes somewhat normal, predictable or calm, you may create a problem to get back to the lower vibration that feels more familiar. So, when you are feeling very balanced and holding a high vibration, what are the subtle ways that you bring yourself back to your original state? Perhaps you begin to drink alcohol, start a fight or eat unhealthily. Maybe you call a person that you know will hurt you or you put yourself in harm's way. The most powerful thing an alchemist can do is become a Master of the chaos within. This power arises when you quickly identify the ways that you sabotage your own success, and decide not to make the same mistake again. When you do this, your energetic vibration begins to rise.

CHAPTER SEVEN: DISTILLATION

YOUR DEEPEST DESIRES

This is the phase of alchemy that marks the final death of your old way of being and your egoic self so you can be born into your new life during the next stage — the Coagulation stage — where it all comes together. Distillation is full surrender to the Divine and a release of personal or selfish drives in the creation process. You will stop pushing through life in a domineering way, and learn to completely relax and trust that there is a bigger plan at work. Distillation helps the alchemist understand how their microcosmic view of the world is related to the macrocosm of the Universe. By this point, you are aware that the mind will manifest in form, but this is the phase where time and space collapse, and visions are manifested much faster. When this happens, you will see just how accurately your thoughts and words create your world. Normally there is a delay in the creation, but in the Distillation phase, there is not.

This occurs so that the alchemist can see just how powerful the mind is and decide to stop creating from this projected level of reality. A massive shift begins as you move your attention from manifesting from the level of the mind to the level of the heart. A deep surrender takes place at the end of Distillation. One will move into a state of being rather than doing. Thoughts dissipate and the world is experienced as it should be — through presence. This experience allows a great amount of peace, spaciousness, and love to flow through.

All of your instincts and stubborn belief systems must be purified for this shift to take place. The mind becomes pressurized and steamed by a higher power for final purification. Archetypal images, Masters and Sages may enter your visions and waking reality in order to help you through these stages of release. The Distillation process clears emotional chaos so that you can move fully into the energy of love and compassion. Hauck says, "The purest experience of emotional energy (such as love) is sometimes found where it is least expected — in unattachment. This separation or distancing from the object of desire allows an entirely new perspective."[3] By the end of Distillation, your consciousness will be turned inward in total surrender to God's will. The alchemist will finally release their deepest desires and see that there is a bigger plan at work for their life. The rise of the Phoenix can then occur and a new way of Being is birthed onto this planet.

LET GO AND LET GOD

During my phase of Distillation, I was meditating for longer periods of time and my visions came to life with great intensity. I began to realize that my mind could create whatever it wanted, but until I was at peace internally, I would continually be unsatisfied with what I was creating in the outside world. If you let a man (or anything outside yourself) make you happy, tomorrow he will make you sad. Make yourself happy and you will always be happy. It was in this stage of transformation that I recognized that the love I craved had to come from me. I was focused on getting a relationship by pushing to make it happen rather than receive. When I finally surrendered, this book began to flow through at a faster rate and what was once just an outline became words made into art as I recognized how The Great Work constructs reality.

I am now going to describe various internal visions that came to life before my eyes. Describing internal visions in a book does not give this fifth dimensional world the credit it deserves, but I will do the best that I can. When visions are created for me, I experience them like a movie across my forehead. I am able to see in color, smelling, feeling, and becoming fully enveloped by many of these shamanic experiences. This is similar to what some have named astral traveling, where the subtle body of the individual leaves to go to a different location where the person can fully experience the environment as if he or she were really there.

The following happened over a period of a few months. After my Fermentation stage, I began to psychically go up and down the vertical access of reality, experiencing the "as above, so below" state, where, as I have previously mentioned, you begin to subtly exist both on Earth and in higher dimensional fields simultaneously. The Universe began to manifest my desires and inner world before my eyes. Personally, I experienced this through dating or relationship with another. As an alchemist, you may have an entirely different experience in Distillation, or other phases of alchemy that meet your psychological needs for change. But the same result happens for all alchemists at the end of Distillation, which is surrender and letting go of personal desire in order to co-create with what the Universe desires.

After I met the man in the park, I helped him to heal and taught him many meditations that changed his life. We became friends — not lifelong partners. I then went on to casually date a few more men over time. I had healed the part of me that attracted dangerous men, but there was still some aspect of me that was attracting men that needed healing. I had more healing to do and was receiving this reflected back to me through relationship. I was also experiencing just how magical the Distillation period of growth is. I will do my best to describe a couple of dates that I went on and how the Universe came through.

THE SIKH MAN

The Kundalini Yoga heritage works with the Sikh Masters, including Guru Ram Das, Yogi Bhajan, and Guru Nanek. As you continue your journey of awakening, you will experience many teachers on Earth that enter your life to guide you through your hero's journey. You will also begin to experience the Ascended Masters from the Heavenly realms. When you pray to a Master or Sage from any lineage, they will respond through dreams, visions, or manifesting in form to help you solve your problems. I had been praying to Guru Ram Das to help heal me and bring me my life partner for two years. Over this period, he came to me very clearly through dreams, explaining what I had to heal within first, including helping me to find more self-love and showing me the ways that I gave my love away.

One day, he came through a man on a date. I met this man on a dating application online. There were 4,500 men that liked me on this platform, and each had very little description and a couple of photos. The chances of meeting a man with a similar background was slim. We decided to meet in the park for a picnic for our date. When he walked up to me, I saw the most beautiful Indian man I had ever seen. He was glowing and he just so happened to be from the Sikh heritage (the same lineage that the prayers and meditations I do come from). I manifested a handsome Sikh man on my picnic blanket that was born in the Himalayas and practiced as a doctor and surgeon (out of thousands of men, there he was). He sat down and I looked into his eyes which did not reflect the eyes of a man. I was looking directly at the Beloved and love flowed deeply from my heart.

This man said to me, "I am not your partner, but I am here to tell you that I will help you with absolutely anything. Anything you need, I am here for you. Always." I realized that though I was sitting with a man, I was also experiencing the Divine speak through this man. When you move into your heart, you begin to hear and experience the Beloved, or God, in everything and everyone. I called my friends who knew my journey and told them, "I just met Guru Ram Das on my date!". We laughed, but they knew I was serious. I was beginning to merge with The One. I became friends with this man and at various times through our friendship, the Beloved would come through and speak to me, answering specific questions that I asked silently through prayer.

You may remember that earlier in the book I mentioned that birds were the symbol that represented relationship for me; I also coincidentally had a pair of pet birds. After meeting him, I opened the cage for my two little birds so they could complete their morning flight around the room. I didn't notice the tiny crack in the window, and my female bird flew away. She left her male counterpart in the cage. Birds are not only a representation of the alchemical process, but they also allow consciousness to work through them. When this bird flew away, I was shocked and yet I understood she was showing me that I was finally ascending. I was leaving the cage of my past behind. Over this period of time, I also made the symbol of three birds on a piece of paper to represent the relationship I wanted to create. The Universe always hears our desires and works through people to respond. After this, a friend sent me the song by Bob Marley called "Three Little Birds," not knowing this was my symbol. I listened to the song over the next couple of weeks and sang along.

THE EAST COAST PREPPY MAN

As I continued through the Distillation phase, more shamanic-like experiences were coming to fruition. Months prior I had experienced a vision that showed me that the relationship I was searching for was actually the book I was going to be writing, though I did not understand this at the time. In that vision, I saw the Goddess of Love, Venus, rise from the water and hand me a ruby necklace. Then I saw myself sitting on a lake with swans, under trees on a white chair writing my book on my laptop. I visualized the man I was hoping to find, standing at the side of the chair, dressed in what looked like "east coast preppy style," calmly watching me write.

I took a trip to Connecticut out of the blue with my children and a girlfriend, who offered to drive us. On the car ride out of the city, I read that Venus was showing herself in the skies and I saw a picture of the Goddess Venus rising from the water. This looked just like the vision I had received months prior. We continued driving, with no specific destination in mind in Connecticut, and ended up at a beach. When we arrived, a friend sent me a movie with an interesting plotline of a woman who received a ruby necklace and found her true love. I was a little stunned by receiving this. I told my friend that I believed my vision from months past was manifesting, and asked her to walk along the beach with me and my children. I knew for sure we would find a white Nantucket-style chair underneath trees near swans. Sure enough, there was the chair and the swans (they are the symbol of Distillation). I sat down on the chair and pulled out my computer to continue to write this book. Where was the man in the vision, though?

Turns out the man I was meeting that night to go on a date just so happened to be from Connecticut. The night before this date, I was speaking to my Beloved (which represented the man I hoped to date) internally and I saw him handing me earth, or dirt, from the ground. When my date from Connecticut arrived, he was dressed in east coast preppy style clothing and he brought me herbs, planted in soil in a pot. My internal and external worlds were beginning to melt together. Though we had a wonderful time together, this man lost his job a couple of days after meeting me and needed time to get his life back together.

The next morning, I was telling my friend about the date, explaining that I liked him but was generally worried and couldn't tell why yet. Out of nowhere, three little birds came to my apartment doorstep and then walked around inside the church. My friend knew about my symbol and the song. Just as my sister had done when the bird arrived at her window when my dad died, I turned on the video on my phone to show my friend the birds so she could witness this miracle too. We both began to sing the lyrics of "Three Little Birds."

Rise up this mornin'
Smile with the risin' sun
Three little birds
Pitch by my doorstep
Singin' sweet songs
Of melodies pure and true
Sayin', this is my message to you
Singin', don't worry 'bout a thing
'Cause every little thing gonna be alright
Singin', don't worry 'bout a thing
Cause every little thing gonna be alright.

SURRENDER

To be in love with some-thing or some-one, is a wildly popular myth. People talk about falling in love and being in love. What about being, IN love. With Everyone. With Every-

thing. All of Creation. Existence. Life Itself. To be in love. To be, IN Love, is to be ONE.

— Manpreet Kaur

During Distillation, the alchemist begins to understand that The One can be found within every person and situation if you can find the Beloved within. The experiences I have just described were the psychic forces required to create the last agitation within me to fully release my personal desire to find The One through a male. These dating experiences showed me that I could clearly create the future, but I was creating a future based on personal desires — and not co-creating with the One Mind to create a future based on what was truly meant for me. Hauck explains in the Emerald Tablet that in order to enter into the One Mind, or mind of God, the alchemist cannot have base emotions. He or she must be completely purified from passion to comingle with the Holy Spirit and move fully into the light. This means that the egoic mind must let go of the most precious personal desires to begin to serve the Beloved One.

For a few days, I thought the man that offered me the plant was my partner, because, my God, how could he have known this was my symbol? And what about those birds appearing at my door, wasn't that a clear sign he was The One? No, these were just manifestations of my inner world manifesting in the outer world. I realized at this point that, rather than co-create on a personal level, it was time to co-create on a Universal level. I am an alchemist, and with this comes responsibility (repeat that out loud). I understood that something bigger was trying to be birthed through me. This made me drop my personal desire to be in a relationship and serve a greater purpose. I let go of the human story in that moment and wrote this book within weeks. The end of the Distillation phase of the alchemical process cleared my thoughts enough to allow the flow of energy to come through me with ease.

Being in relationship can be very healing, as the other person reflects the parts of you that still need work. As I have discussed, once these aspects of yourself and original wounds are healed, you will no longer need this reflection. The person will either begin to heal to the same level as you or leave your life because your frequencies don't match and you are no longer bonding over similar wounds. The final aspect of healing my original wound required a period of self-reflection. If I continued to try and heal these men, I was avoiding my own healing.

When we spend our whole life putting a significant amount of thought and energy into something outside of ourselves, we lose our own identity and the truth of who we are. I realized that I had been in relationship with a man since I was sixteen years old. Even after I left my husband, I was still searching for The One, always hoping that someone else could give me love. Original wounds cannot live in the vibration of self-generated love. It was time to love myself and put my energy into something meaningful that more people could benefit from.

The healing of your original wounds will first ignite a sense of anger and shock that you were so badly hurt. You may mourn for some time and then become disorganized as you begin to reorganize your psyche. When you have spent your entire life unconsciously focused on these thoughts, what do you do with your time and energy when they no longer exist? I want you to begin to consider how much time you have spent worrying about others, how you have allowed yourself to be hurt, and just how much you have hurt yourself. Self-reflect on the amount of energy you have expended thinking about your weight, if someone likes you, or if your work is worthy of praise. When you stop putting your energy out in so many chaotic and destructive directions, you have a lot left for yourself.

Self-love begins to accumulate when you take all the energy you were putting into an outside source back into you. If you drink too much alcohol, do drugs, excessively work out, fight with others or gossip, you are losing valuable time here on Earth. As self-destruction fades away, creativity can pour through. The Universe has so much energy and it is always looking for a vessel to enter. Once you begin to fill yourself up with love that is not needed from an outside source, the Universe will see itself reflected through you and reinvigorate your life. When mental thoughts stop focusing on past wounds and projecting how the future will create happiness, the energy of the present moment is birthed.

My desire was draining all of my power. Personal desire possesses the mind, and when the possession fades and when you free your mind, you will begin to think clearly and have spaces in between thought. Desire in general is an energy vampire that takes us further away from fully receiving. I had to let go of the outcome, and when I did, my way of Being did too. I let go of needing a particular result and my obsessive attachment to it. When I stopped being self-serving, the Universe saw that there was space to birth something creative through me. I had spent my entire life unconsciously projecting my wound, and once I surrendered, everything changed. My work became empowered and so did I.

CHAPTER EIGHT: COAGULATION

A LEGACY OF LOVE

Coagulation brings a calm and centered space of reflection into the alchemist's life. Hauck said, "Psychologically, the Phoenix is the resurrected personality seen as a successful individuation resulting in peace of mind, heightened energy, and free-flowing adaptability to new situations. The alchemist remembers inspired states of Fermentation and Distillation and has made them a permanent part of his personality. He deliberately slows down his pace of life to allow feelings and intuition to surface. In this way, he stays connected to a newly discovered Presence within."[4] This is the point that the archetype on the hero's journey returns home with the secret elixir of life which is Presence, and the vibration that comes with the state of Being.

The hero reflects on the long journey he or she has been on and begins to see how much knowledge and energy has been accumulated. The secret elixir also brings a new outlook on life, confidence, and the destruction of mental issues that once plagued him or her.

This is the point where your trauma is healed and you are no longer playing out the story of the past. If you have been functioning from an unawakened state and have been controlled by your mind for most of your life, getting to this stage in alchemical transformation is similar to becoming an entirely new human being. It may be the first time when real peace is felt. Life unfolds between order and chaos. Each time you lean towards one extreme, you will create the other in your life. Staying in the middle is the way to create the Presence that arises during the stage of Coagulation. The alchemist learns to go with the flow of life with great acceptance. There is a sense of awe and inspiration that is consecrated into the individual from the previous stages, but no agitation. Life is taken step by step and moment by moment, as pushing or negativity is healed now.

A coagulated human being is psychologically, emotionally, mentally, and spiritually integrated. They know themselves. The past and the future no longer dictate their life, so there is less turmoil and more clarity. The individual knows what they are feeling in each moment and can manage the emotions through observation and not reaction. The Presence that is gained through these moments of silent truth creates what the Emerald Tablet refers to as The Stone. This is a solidified and non-reactive state, which produces one of the most powerful creative tools on Earth — the human mind connected to the One Mind. When an individual's mind is no longer controlled by outside opinions or the mental chaos of the world, he or she completely separates from the controlled matrix on Earth. The process of fully awakening is liberation from the mind.

When the alchemist is no longer stuck in their trauma from the past or worried about a future that has not happened, a great amount of creativity and love can flow through. In this state of joy, each alchemist will produce a unique signature for the planet. They create something legendary and long-lasting. Some alchemists may write books, some may make music, and others may create love just through their vibration. The inner journey the alchemist goes through transforms everyone around them. Through this refined frequency, the alchemist becomes grounded on Earth with their heart and mind open to the sky.

They are able to do this because they have found their inner treasure and understand their soul is connected to the soul of the Universe. When an individual becomes connected in this way, various types of ideas, poetry, art, relationships, and even children, can be birthed that have never been seen on this planet before. This is a level of sovereignty that is very rare, and with it comes the ability to ignore outside noise and follow the omens that the Universe provides. An alchemist learns to stop comparing their creativity to what others are creating, they do not let the news dictate their thoughts, and they live their life from a very deep inner knowing and trust.

The greatest teachers, healers, artists, and enlightened Beings, including Buddha, Mary Magdalene and Jesus, completed the alchemical journey. Each of these Masters made a unique signature on Earth and through many dimensions; we can call it their legacy of love. They are legends that exceed the limits of time and space. This is the secret of the eighth step in alchemy — manifesting a vibration and archetype that has a unique story which can help others to awaken too. Their unique archetypal pathways to enlightenment help the collective to find the same Divine Love that these unique Beings experienced in their own lives. This is what Hauck refers to as the *Signature of God* in the Emerald Tablet. It is the essence of the heart and the mystical experience of seeking God and Divine Love in every moment. The intention to produce something that is creative — and not destructive — with your mind is one of the greatest achievements for a human being. Whether this is a poem, a garden, a positive vibration, an act of goodwill or art, you are focused on improving the environment around you. Each of us can individually awaken humanity through these acts of love.

MOVING INTO PRESENCE

During my Coagulation phase, I took a significant amount of time to reflect on how far I had come in my life. I had been pushing for so long, thinking that, by finding The One through a partner, I would feel healed. The greatest moment of awakening I ever experienced was when I finally let go of all of my resistance to internal peace. The thoughts that had haunted me my whole life disappeared. My story disintegrated. Though my mind would sometimes slip into the past and occasionally in to the future, this occurred less and less during the stage of Coagulation. My attention went into my Self and my overall body energy, which was increasing in vibratory speed daily. I felt less of an urge to do and realized how much unnecessary activity had once consumed my life.

Anytime I began to be taken away from my state of comfort, I questioned the activity. I saw that addiction to anything outside myself created anxiety. Excess in any form became apparent, especially through alcohol, technology, social media, or gatherings. I began to notice more and more where my energy was going and became content and contained — which made me more receptive and intuitive. I did what was necessary and was healing my inner masculine or internal father figure through the process. I no longer needed this outside male figure to love me because I began to love and appreciate myself. My activities became conscious and not compulsive. I got on the train to go to work and enjoyed my job immensely at the fertility clinic. I came home and walked, then enjoyed my time with my children and select friends. I also wrote and edited this book.

You may be thinking, "Well that sounds like life." Not for me though. I had never lived a life that was not chaotic and echoing the insanity of my thoughts back at me. I recognized that my life had been lived at hyperspeed. I had always made school, work, kids, and travel complicated and busy. I enjoyed a packed schedule, but internally complained about it. I never moved consciously enough within my body to actually enjoy — to be in joy with — what was happening. I was now no longer living from the level of my mind, but from my heart. My mind was not controlled on a personal level by my past or affected on a societal level by what was happening in the news. I started to question any thoughts that arose in my mind — questioning them for truth. I realized that if I didn't love my thoughts, I couldn't love my life, because they were one. Self-love that is this radical in nature is like a sword and a shield. It is your personal army and protective force against the masses that suffer from destructive thoughts and self-hate.

Your world is birthed through your mind, and understanding this is the most humbling experience a human can go through because there is no one outside of yourself to blame anymore. Recognize that if there is a war in your house, you started it or are keeping it going by resisting change. I had been searching for The One, not consciously realizing that it is all One. I was only dealing with aspects of myself projected back at me and this dream could be a nightmare or a beautiful fantasy. Byron Katie, author of *A Mind at Home with Itself*, described this well when she said, "You are who you believe you are. Other people are, for you, who you believe they are; they can be nothing more than that. If you realized that the mind is one, that everyone and everything is your own projection (including you), you would understand that it is only yourself you are ever dealing with. You would end up loving yourself, loving every thought you think. When you love every thought, you love everything thoughts create, you love the whole world you have created." [5]

Eckhart Tolle said in his book *The Power of Now*, "Choice begins the moment you disidentify from the mind and its conditioned patterns, the moment you become present. Until you reach this point, you are unconscious, spiritually speaking. This means that you are compelled to think, feel, and act in certain ways according to the conditioning of your mind."[6] I remember reading Tolle's work years before I started my alchemical journey, and I could not understand anything he was saying. Not a word. I repeatedly listened to his lectures, hoping that some aspect of his ability to be present would come through to me. At that time, I didn't clearly understand just how intense the journey to even taste what he was talking about would be.

I also could not have fathomed that, when we are unconscious, we don't have a choice to not repeat the past. Jesus said, "Forgive them, for they know not what they do." The majority of individuals on this planet are living completely unconsciously, meaning they are unaware of themselves and the dream around them. To put this in the perspective of the concept of the original wound I have discussed in this book, I was not even conscious of the amount of peace I could feel until I awakened to my heart. I was not aware of the fact that I had not had a healthy relationship with a man until I began to heal and awaken to the fact that things could be different. I was stuck recreating the past with every man I met in my life because I had no choice. Until humanity becomes aware of their original wounds, they will not awaken either.

Tolle said, "Nobody chooses dysfunction, conflict, pain. Nobody chooses insanity. They happen because there is not enough presence in you to dissolve the past, not enough light to dispel the darkness. You are not fully here. You have not quite woken up yet. In the meantime, the conditioned mind is running your life."[7] Aha! There is a way out and it is through the present moment. I was being controlled by a mental and emotional pattern dictated by my past and compelled to try to change it through future projections, yet my only peace could be found right where I was at — the present moment. Breaking from my original wounds, which were generational, took deep reprogramming and the release of past conditions and limited belief systems of what is possible. The process of healing your original wounds will require the same from you.

If there is a part of you that feels a discomfort within — a feeling that you have not completed what you came here to do or a knowing that there must be more here on Earth — look to your original wounds and allow yourself to grow from there. Go through the darkness of your maddening thoughts to get to the light. Through this light, you will touch into your creative birthright and the aspects of you that are typically numbed or stifled. You have put down the weight of your past to see the present as it is — happening now.

BECOMING WHOLE

Through Coagulation, I learned that everything you need comes from the relationship you have with yourself. Becoming whole means becoming contained in your energy field, committed to your personal growth, and content with your life. It is returning to the state of the ouroboros snake. I needed to become self-reliant and sustaining in my own love. A woman in her power can be self-generating and self-renewing. Like a fountain that continues to regenerate its own water, or a snake that eats its own tail — this is my love. As women, if we look to a male, or anything outside of ourselves on this plane of existence for our happiness, we fall from grace. God or Spirit must be our first source of energy because it is never-ending. We must learn to rely on cosmic energy. This is The One I had always been searching for and I experienced this serenity and immense grace during the alchemical steps of transformation.

Much of what I had been looking for within a man was carnal in nature and was based in desire. The word 'woman' contains the word 'man,' and the word 'she' contains 'he.' I realized that, because women create men, if we are looking to them to make us content, we are essentially looking for separated parts of ourselves to become whole again. A whole person has healed both the masculine and feminine aspects within — the father and the mother wounds. Reuniting comes from going within. I could see clearly that the outer world could not be my source of comfort. A relationship could not be my source of comfort. My connection to Source became my only source of comfort and everything flowed from this. If women are not in their sovereignty, they will never be truly at peace or happy.

When you are initiated into this kind of rare and unique energy on the planet, the men around you will be initiated too. The males in your life will be asked to step into manhood, if they have not already, and raise their vibration to meet you where you are at. If they are unable to do this, they will not be able to energetically last within your new vibrational frequency, meaning they will not be the right partner or even friend for you. As a collective, we must hold space for this energetic shift to happen because this is how the patriarchy will heal. We cannot heal through anger or fighting what already is, but we can heal through raising consciousness.

AWAKENING TO SOVEREIGNTY

The process of awakening is not always an easy path. As humans, we currently require some kind of opposing force to help us find ourselves. This is the law of polarity. In order to know who we are, we must know who we are not. Most of us do not even remember what we are looking for, or truly understand who we are inside, because there are so many layers that separate us from our True Selves or from Source. Throughout this book, I have referenced these layers of pain and trauma as our original wounds. On the path to securing a healthy relationship, we must peel away all of the unhealthy parts of ourselves. It requires deep introspection and the ability to locate patterns from our past that sneak into the present. In order to open the heart, we have to face our greatest wounds and deprogram what our families, society, and culture have taught us to be true. We have to free ourselves to become self-sovereign.

I always had a difficult time pronouncing the word sovereignty until now, and maybe this is because no one ever taught me what it was. We do not have many tangible examples of what it means to be sovereign on the planet, but to me it means the liberation of the mind and the opening of the heart center. Sovereignty is a state of autonomy. It is self-governing. Now, more than ever, we must begin to cultivate this state of freedom and liberation within or risk being controlled by outside forces that would prefer we stay in the lower vibrations of trauma, pain, and fear. The process of gaining self-sovereignty on the path to awakening is the hero's journey of releasing all of the internal and external forms that attempt to control us and separate us from our own power. This not only permeates our personal relationships, but also our society, culture, and government. Anything that keeps you small or unworthy on the path to crowning yourself with this kind of freedom must be released.

Diving into our original wounds feels heartbreaking, but in order for humanity to move into the next level of accelerated growth, each of us will have to go through our own heart-opening experiences. To do this, we have to move through whatever energies the heart has been holding onto that has hindered its full opening. These emotions include sadness, heartbreak, anger, attachment, depression, loneliness, or grief. The releasing of these layers of emotions requires you to actually feel them and sometimes re-experience them. It seems counterintuitive to have to experience fear in order to feel love, or experience grief in order to know joy, but again, we cannot find out who we are until we know who we are not. The key to the process is not getting stuck in these lower vibrational experiences. The important part is letting go and raising our consciousness enough to create a new world that is not repeating the past. We can do this by using the spiritual technologies mentioned in this book, in *Mystical Motherhood* and *Fertile*, or through other sources that may be more applicable to your situation.

When you become sovereign in your thoughts, your destiny will be revealed through your connection to Spirit or The One. You become an alchemist with the power of transmuting energy. Through your transformation, you will become magnetic, receptive, contained, content, and graceful, which are the qualities of the Divine Feminine. You will also become discerning, grounded, and know when to take the right action and when to hold back your energy, which are the qualities of the Divine Masculine. In a world that easily crumbles externally, how can you stay steady and centered and in your own Divine Love? Your source of love must come from the inside and from here you will co-create a new reality on Earth.

YOUR JOURNEY BACK HOME

Since the beginning of the book, I have discussed the stages of the hero's journey in conjunction with the stages of alchemical transformation that lie on the path to awakening. The alchemist is thrust into this evolutionary journey as the elements begin to transform consciousness, in order for the Soul to merge with the Soul of the Universe, or The One. You may personally be at the beginning of this journey or at the end. If you are at the beginning, the chaos of your thoughts, or the desire of your soul's evolution to accelerate your growth, will push you forward to make internal changes. Your personal transformation will then begin to radically change your outside world.

This is when the call to action may arrive. This is the moment that requires great courage, as you will be invited to go against old belief systems, society's traditional ways, and your family's generational history. The leap in consciousness will require you to move through and far beyond your original wounds, which hold you locked within a false matrix on this planet. Through this process, you will be called to follow your heart's navigation system and the omens that lead you to your highest destiny. Your call to action may not be as dramatic as leaving your entire life behind, but even small changes go a very long way on the road to awakening. When the elements begin to create transformation, it often feels like you are getting hit from all directions.

Fire moves into your life to burn away all that does not belong and release the attachments of your ego. Water challenges your emotional capacity to function and requires that you learn self-regulation. Air forces your thoughts to become pure through mental agitation. Earth helps to ground you into your new life and build a foundation that lasts. Ether allows you to connect into the higher realms while on Earth, and bring back new knowledge that will benefit humanity as a whole. The elements create hurdles in order to balance the alchemist physically, mentally, emotionally, and spiritually.

Fear arises as you work through the wounds that keep you stuck in old patterns and unable to develop further in life. It takes courage to change and you will face many internal and external obstacles. Along the alchemical journey, you will learn to navigate signs from the Universe. Sometimes signs are used as warning signals and sometimes they lead you to your next best step. It takes time and practice to begin to trust your internal navigation system. On the hero's journey, you will also learn to navigate danger, which will come in the form of people and environments that are toxic. This will help you gain insight into who is trustworthy — and human character in general. A metaphysical death occurs that will eventually transform you fully into the alchemist who is resurrected and rewarded with a new life.

This is what happened to me at least: my journey grounded me into a brand-new life. As I write this now, I am in my new home which just so happens to be on Greene Avenue. This symbolically represents the Emerald Tablet. I wrote two books in the temple or church on Adelphi Street that I was guided to move to after visiting the Great Pyramid in Egypt. I do not believe that I could have energetically birthed these books in any other location on Earth.

In fact, I was always wondering why I was asked to move to this specific location and then I heard a story that caught my attention about another author. While watching a video produced by Eckhart Tolle, he said that he had made a prayer to the Universe. It was a prayer to awaken humanity — similar to mine. He wrote his prayer on a piece of paper, folded it, and put it away. His mind then became obsessed with the thoughts of moving from England to a small town in California. He had never been to this location in California and he didn't know anyone there, but the little voice inside him wouldn't go away and his heart was navigating his destiny.

He followed that voice not knowing why and ended up writing the books *A New Earth* and *The Power of Now*, in a specific home that he was guided to in California. He explained that when he tried to leave this location, he could not write his books, as the energy did not flow anywhere else. Watching this video gave me a better understanding as to why I was led to go to Brooklyn and find that Temple where I would heal. I am so glad that I listened to that voice inside. I am not comparing my work to his; I only include this story as a reference to a fellow alchemist who followed a call to action. His story is a potent reminder of the power of prayer. As an alchemist, you now know that your thoughts matter, your prayer counts and places of power are important for your growth.

While in that church, I found the gold that every alchemist is looking for. I found myself and my Unique Signature in relation to the One Source. I discovered the guiding light of my heart. I healed the original wounds of my past so that I could move forward in a better life for myself and my children. The gold I found is the gift of this book, which will help you find your gold too. This is the power of alchemy. It transforms everything around it.

Works Cited

Brown, S. L. (2005). *How to Spot a Dangerous Man Before You Get Involved.* Alameda: Hunter House Publications.

Hauck, D. W. (1999). *The Emerald Tablet: Alchemy for Personal Transformation.* New York City: Penguin Books.

Heller, A. L. (2010). *Attached: The New Science of Adult Attachment and How It Can Help You Find — and Keep — Love.* Penguin Random House.

Katie, B. (2018). *A Mind at Home with Itself: How Asking Four Questions Can Free Your Mind, Open Your Heart, and Turn Your World Around.* New York City: Harper One.

Tolle, E. (1999). *The Power of Now: A Guide to Spiritual Enlightenment.* Vancouver: The New World Library.

Tolle, E. (2003). *A New Earth: Awakening to Your Life's Purpose.* New York: Penguin Books.

Walsch, N. D. (2017). *Conversations With God, Book 4: Awaken the Species.* Faber, Virginia: Rainbow Ridge Books.

End Notes

1. (Hauck, 1999)
2. (Hauck, 1999)
3. (Hauck, 1999)
4. (Hauck, 1999)
5. (Katie, 2018)
6. (Tolle E. , 2003)
7. (Tolle E. , 2003)

www.ingramcontent.com/pod-product-compliance
Lightning Source LLC
Chambersburg PA
CBHW070303010526
44108CB00039B/1648